BIBLE READINGS
for Boys and Girls

Selected Passages from the
Revised Standard Version of the Holy Bible
Illustrated by Lynd Ward

Bible. English. Selections. 1959. Revised standard.

THOMAS NELSON & SONS

Edinburgh   NEW YORK   Toronto

Here is a book prepared especially for boys and girls. It contains passages selected from the Bible to help you to know some of the people, ideas, and events in this most important of all books. As you read these selections, you may wish to turn to the Bible itself to find out more about what it says. To help you to do this, references are given at the end of each section.

The pictures will tell you a great deal about Bible times and places. As you study them, they may also help you to catch the Bible's message for your own life.

The preparation of this book has brought great joy to a number of people. They hope that reading it will bring great joy to you, too.

Table of Contents

Old Testament

In the Beginning

In the beginning God created the heavens and the earth. The earth was without form and void, and darkness was upon the face of the deep; and the Spirit of God was moving over the face of the waters.

And God said, "Let there be light"; and there was light. And God saw that the light was good; and God separated the light from the darkness. God called the light Day, and the darkness he called Night. And there was evening and there was morning, one day.

And God said, "Let there be a firmament in the midst of the waters, and let it separate the waters from the waters." And God made the firmament and separated the waters which were under the firmament from the waters which were above the firmament. And it was so. And God called the firmament Heaven. And there was evening and there was morning, a second day.

And God said, "Let the waters under the heavens be gathered together into one place, and let the dry land appear." And it was so. God called the dry land Earth, and the waters that were gathered together he called

Seas. And God saw that it was good. And God said, "Let the earth put forth vegetation, plants yielding seed, and fruit trees bearing fruit in which is their seed, each according to its kind, upon the earth." And it was so. The earth brought forth vegetation, plants yielding seed according to their own kinds, and trees bearing fruit in which is their seed, each according to its kind. And God saw that it was good. And there was evening and there was morning, a third day.

And God said, "Let there be lights in the firmament of the heavens to separate the day from the night; and let them be for signs and for seasons and for days and years, and let them be lights in the firmament of the heavens to

give light upon the earth." And it was so. And God made the two great lights, the greater light to rule the day, and the lesser light to rule the night; he made the stars also. And God set them in the firmament of the heavens to give light upon the earth, to rule over the day and over the night, and to separate the light from the darkness. And God saw that it was good. And there was evening and there was morning, a fourth day.

And God said, "Let the waters bring forth swarms of living creatures, and let birds fly above the earth across the firmament of the heavens." So God created the great sea monsters and every living creature that moves, with which the waters swarm, according to their kinds, and every winged bird according to its kind. And God saw that it was good. And God blessed them, saying, "Be fruitful and multiply and fill the waters in the seas, and let birds multiply on the earth." And there was evening and there was morning, a fifth day.

And God said, "Let the earth bring forth living creatures according to their kinds: cattle and creeping things and beasts of the earth according to their kinds." And it was so. And God made the beasts of the earth according to their kinds and the cattle according to their kinds, and everything that creeps upon the ground according to its kind. And God saw that it was good.

Then God said, "Let us make man in our image, after our likeness; and let them have dominion over the fish of the sea, and over the birds of the air, and over the cattle, and over all the earth, and over every creeping thing that creeps upon the earth." So God created man in his own image, in the image of God he created him; male and female he created them. And God blessed them, and God said to them, "Be fruitful and multiply, and fill the earth and subdue it; and have dominion over the fish of the sea and over the birds of the air and over every living thing that moves upon the earth." And God said, "Behold, I have given you every plant yielding seed which is upon the face of all the earth, and every tree with seed in its fruit; you shall have them for food. And to every beast of the earth and to every bird of the air, and to everything that creeps on the earth, everything that has the breath of life, I have given every green plant for food." And it was so. And God saw everything that he had made, and behold, it was very good. And there was evening and there was morning, a sixth day.

Thus the heavens and the earth were finished, and all the host of them. And on the seventh day God finished his work which he had done, and he rested on the seventh day from all his work which he had done. So God blessed the seventh day and hallowed it, because on it God rested from all his work in creation.

From Genesis 1: 1–31; 2: 1–3.

The Garden of Eden

And the LORD God planted a garden in Eden, in the east; and there he put the man whom he had formed. And out of the ground the LORD God made to grow every tree that is pleasant to the sight and good for food, the tree of life also in the midst of the garden, and the tree of the knowledge of good and evil.

Then the LORD God said, "It is not good that the man should be alone; I will make him a helper fit for him." And God made a woman and brought her to the man.

And Adam called his wife's name Eve, because she was the mother of all living.

And the LORD God commanded the man, saying, "You may freely eat of every tree of the garden; but of the tree of the knowledge of good and evil you shall not eat." Now the serpent was more subtle than any other

wild creature that the LORD God had made. He said to the woman, "Did God say, 'You shall not eat of any tree of the garden'?" And the woman said to the serpent, "We may eat of the fruit of the trees of the garden; but God said, 'You shall not eat of the fruit of the tree which is in the midst of the garden, neither shall you touch it, lest you die.'" But the serpent said to the woman, "You will not die. For God knows that when you eat of it your eyes will be opened, and you will be like God, knowing good and evil." When the woman saw that the tree was good for food, and was to be desired to make one wise, she took of its fruit and ate; and gave some to her husband, and he ate.

But the LORD God called to the man, and said to him, "Where are you?" And he said, "I heard the sound of thee in the garden, and I was afraid. The woman whom thou gavest to be with me, she gave me fruit of the tree,

13

and I ate." Then the Lord God said to the woman, "What is this that you have done?" The woman said, "The serpent beguiled me, and I ate."

Therefore the Lord God sent them forth from the garden of Eden.

From Genesis 2: 8–9, 18, 22; 3: 20; 2: 16–17; 3: 1–6, 9–10, 12–13, 22, 23.

God's Covenant with Noah

When men began to multiply on the face of the ground, the Lord saw that the wickedness of man was great in the earth. And the Lord was sorry that he had made man on the earth, and it grieved him to his heart.

But Noah found favor in the eyes of the Lord. Noah was a righteous man, blameless in his generation. And Noah had three sons, Shem, Ham, and Japheth.

And God said to Noah, "Make yourself an ark of gopher wood; make rooms in the ark, and cover it inside

14

and out with pitch. You shall come into the ark, you, your sons, your wife, and your sons' wives with you. And of every living thing of all flesh, you shall bring two of every sort into the ark, to keep them alive with you; they shall be male and female. Also take with you every sort of food that is eaten, and store it up."

And Noah and his sons and his wife and his sons' wives with him went into the ark. And after seven days the waters of the flood came upon the earth. The flood continued forty days upon the earth; and the waters increased, and bore up the ark, and it rose high above the earth. And the waters prevailed so mightily upon the earth that all the high mountains were covered.

But God remembered Noah and all that were with him in the ark. And God made a wind blow, and the waters subsided; the ark came to rest upon Ar'arat.

15

Noah went forth, and his sons and his wife and his sons' wives with him and every beast, every creeping thing, and every bird.

Then Noah built an altar to the LORD, and the LORD said, "While the earth remains, seedtime and harvest, cold and heat, summer and winter, day and night, shall not cease.

"I establish my covenant with you, that never again shall there be a flood to destroy the earth. This is the sign of the covenant which I make between me and you for all future generations: I set my bow in the cloud, and it shall be a sign of the covenant."

From Genesis 6: 1, 5–6, 8–10, 13–14, 18–19, 21; 7: 7, 10, 17, 19; 8: 1, 4, 18–22; 9: 11–13.

Abraham and His Family

Terah, a descendant of Shem, took Abram his son and Lot the son of Haran, his grandson, and Sar'ai his daughter-in-law, his son Abram's wife, and they went forth together from Ur of the Chal'deans to go into the land of Canaan; but when they came to Haran, they settled there and Terah died in Haran.

Now the LORD said to Abram, "Go from your country and your father's house to the land that I will show you. And I will make of you a great nation and bless you and make your name great, so that you will be a blessing."

So Abram went, as the LORD had told him; and Lot went with him. Abram was seventy-five years old when he departed from Haran. And Abram took Sar'ai his wife, and Lot his brother's son, and all their possessions which they had gathered, and the persons that they had gotten in Haran; and they set forth to go to the land of Canaan. When they had come to the land of Canaan, Abram passed through the land to the place at Shechem, to the oak of Moreh. Then the LORD appeared to Abram, and said, "To your descendants I will give this land." So he

17

built there an altar to the LORD. And Abram journeyed on, still going toward the Negeb.

Now Abram was very rich in cattle, in silver, and in gold. And Lot, who went with Abram, also had flocks and herds and tents, so that the land could not support both of them dwelling together; and there was strife between the herdsmen of Abram's cattle and the herdsmen of Lot's cattle.

Then Abram said to Lot, "Let there be no strife between your herdsmen and my herdsmen; for we are kinsmen. Is not the whole land before you? Separate yourself from me. If you take the left hand, then I will go to the right; or if you take the right hand, then I will go to the left." And Lot saw that the Jordan valley was well watered everywhere. So Lot chose for himself all the Jordan valley, and Lot journeyed east; thus they separated from each other. Abram dwelt in the land of Canaan, while Lot dwelt among the cities of the valley.

From Genesis 11: 31–32; 12: 1–2, 4–7, 9; 13: 2, 5–12.

God's Promise to Abraham

The LORD said to Abram, after Lot had separated from him, "Lift up your eyes, and look from the place where you are, northward and southward and eastward and westward; for all the land which you see I will give to you and to your descendants for ever. I will make your descendants as the dust of the earth; so that if one can count the dust of the earth, your descendants also can be counted. Arise, walk through the length and the breadth of the land, for I will give it to you." So Abram moved his tent, and came and dwelt by the oaks of Mamre at Hebron; and there he built an altar to the LORD.

After these things the word of the LORD came to Abram in a vision, "Fear not, Abram, I am your shield; your reward shall be very great." But Abram said, "O Lord GOD, what wilt thou give me, for I continue childless; and a slave born in my house will be my heir." And behold, the word of the LORD came to him, "Your own son shall be your heir." And he brought him outside and

19

said, "Look toward heaven, and number the stars, if you are able to number them." Then the LORD said to Abram, "So shall your descendants be." And he believed the LORD; and he reckoned it to him as righteousness.

And God said to him, "No longer shall your name be Abram, but your name shall be Abraham; for I have made you the father of a multitude of nations. As for Sar'ai your wife, you shall not call her name Sar'ai, but Sarah shall be her name. At the appointed time I will return to you, in the spring, and Sarah shall have a son."

Sarah conceived, and bore Abraham a son in his old age at the time of which God had spoken to him. Abraham called the name of his son, Isaac.

And the child grew, and was weaned; and Abraham made a great feast on the day that Isaac was weaned.

From Genesis 13: 14–18; 15: 1–6; 17: 3, 5, 15; 18: 14; 21: 2, 3, 8.

Jacob and Esau

When Isaac was forty years old he took to wife Rebekah, the daughter of Bethu'el the Aramean of Paddan-aram. And Isaac prayed to the LORD for his wife, because she was barren; and the LORD granted his prayer, and Rebekah his wife conceived.

When her days to be delivered were fulfilled, behold there were twins in her womb. The first came forth; they called his name Esau. Afterward, his brother came forth; his name was called Jacob.

When the boys grew up, Esau was a skilful hunter, a man of the field, while Jacob was a quiet man, dwelling in tents. Isaac loved Esau, because he ate of his game; but Rebekah loved Jacob.

Once when Jacob was boiling pottage, Esau came in

20

from the field, and he was famished. And Esau said to
Jacob, "Let me eat some of that red pottage, for I am
famished!" Jacob said, "First sell me your birthright."
Esau said, "I am about to die; of what use is a birthright
to me?" Jacob said, "Swear to me first." So he swore to
him, and sold his birthright to Jacob. Then Jacob gave
Esau bread and pottage of lentils, and he ate and drank,
and went his way. Thus Esau despised his birthright.

From Genesis 25: 20–21, 24–34.

God's Promise to Jacob

One day Rebekah said to Isaac, "If Jacob marries one
of the women of the land, what good will my life be to
me?" Then Isaac called Jacob and blessed him, and
charged him, "You shall not marry one of the Canaanite
women. Arise, go to Paddan-aram to the house of Bethu'el
your mother's father; and take as wife one of the daughters of Laban your mother's brother. God Almighty bless
you and make you fruitful! May he give the blessing of
Abraham to you and to your descendants with you, that
you may take possession of the land which God gave to
Abraham!" Thus Isaac sent Jacob away.

Then Jacob went on his journey, and came to the land
of the people of the east. As he looked, he saw a well in
the field, and lo, three flocks of sheep lying beside it;

for out of that well the flocks were watered. The stone on the well's mouth was large, and when all the flocks were gathered there, the shepherds would roll the stone from the mouth of the well, and water the sheep.

Jacob said to them, "My brothers, where do you come from?" They said, "We are from Haran." He said to them, "Do you know Laban the son of Nahor?" They said, "We know him." He said to them, "Is it well with him?" They said, "It is well; and see, Rachel his daughter is coming with the sheep!"

When Jacob saw Rachel the daughter of Laban his mother's brother, and the sheep of Laban, Jacob went up and rolled the stone from the well's mouth, and watered the flock. Then Jacob told Rachel that he was her father's kinsman, and that he was Rebekah's son; and she ran and told her father.

When Laban heard the tidings of Jacob his sister's son, he ran to meet him, and embraced him and kissed him, and brought him to his house. Jacob told Laban all these things, and Laban said to him, "Surely you are my bone and my flesh!" And he stayed with him a month.

Now Laban had two daughters; the name of the older was Leah and the name of the younger was Rachel.

Then Laban said to Jacob, "Because you are my kinsman, should you therefore serve me for nothing? Tell me, what shall your wages be?" Jacob loved Rachel; and he said, "I will serve you seven years for your younger daughter Rachel." Laban said, "It is better that I give her to you than that I should give her to any other man; stay with me." So Jacob served seven years for Rachel, and they seemed to him but a few days because of the love he had for her.

Then Jacob said to Laban, "Give me my wife." But

Laban took Leah and brought her to Jacob. And Jacob said to Laban, "What is this you have done to me? Did I not serve with you for Rachel? Why have you deceived me?" Laban said, "It is not so done in our country, to give the younger before the first-born. Complete the week of this one, and we will give you the other also in return for serving me another seven years." Jacob did so. Then Laban gave him Rachel to wife.

Then God remembered Rachel, and she conceived and bore a son, and she called his name Joseph.

Jacob grew exceedingly rich, and had large flocks, maidservants and menservants, and camels and asses.

God appeared to Jacob again, when he came from Paddan-aram, and blessed him. And God said to him, "Your name is Jacob; no longer shall your name be called Jacob, but Israel shall be your name." So his name was called Israel. And God said to him, "I am God Almighty: be fruitful and multiply; a nation and a company of nations shall come from you, and kings shall spring from you. The land which I gave to Abraham and Isaac I will give to you, and I will give the land to your descendants after you." And Jacob set up a pillar in the place where God had spoken with him, a pillar of stone; and he poured out a drink offering on it, and poured oil on it. So Jacob called the name of the place where God had spoken with him, Bethel.

And Jacob came to his father Isaac at Hebron, where Abraham and Isaac had sojourned. Now the days of Isaac were a hundred and eighty years. And Isaac died and was gathered to his people, old and full of days; and his sons Esau and Jacob buried him.

From Genesis 27: 46; 28: 1–5; 29: 1–6, 10–14, 16, 15, 18–21, 23, 25–28; 30: 22–24, 43; 35: 9–12, 14–15, 27–29.

Joseph and His Brothers

Jacob dwelt in the land of his father's sojournings, in Canaan. This is the history of the family of Jacob.

Joseph, being seventeen years old, was shepherding the flock with his older brothers; and Joseph brought an ill report of them to their father. Now Israel loved Joseph more than any other of his children, and he made him a long robe with sleeves. But when his brothers saw that their father loved him more than all his brothers, they hated him, and could not speak peaceably to him.

Now Joseph had a dream, and he told it to his brothers. "Hear this dream: behold, we were binding sheaves in the field, and lo, my sheaf arose and stood upright; and behold, your sheaves gathered round it, and bowed down to my sheaf." His brothers said to him, "Are you indeed to reign over us, or have dominion over us?" So they hated him yet more for his dreams and for his words.

Now his brothers went to pasture their father's flock near Shechem. And Israel said to Joseph, "Are not your brothers pasturing the flock at Shechem? Go now, see if it is well with your brothers, and with the flock; and bring me word again."

So Joseph went after his brothers. They saw him afar off, and before he came near to them they said to one another, "Here comes this dreamer. Come now, let us kill him and throw him into one of the pits; then we shall say that a wild beast has devoured him, and we shall see what will become of his dreams." But when Reuben heard it, he said to them, "Shed no blood; cast him into this pit here in the wilderness, but lay no hand upon Joseph"—that he might rescue him to restore him to his father. So when Joseph came to his brothers, they

stripped him of his robe, the long robe with sleeves that he wore; and they took him and cast him into a pit.

Then they sat down to eat; and looking up they saw a caravan of Ish'maelites coming from Gilead, with their camels bearing gum, balm, and myrrh, on their way to carry it down to Egypt. Then Judah said to his brothers, "What profit is it if we slay our brother and conceal his blood? Come, let us sell him to the Ish'maelites." And his brothers heeded him. Then they drew Joseph up out of the pit, and sold him to the Ish'maelites for twenty shekels of silver; and they took Joseph to Egypt.

From Genesis 37: 1–8, 12–14, 17–28.

Joseph Is Put in Prison

Joseph was taken down to Egypt, and Pot'iphar, an officer of Pharaoh, the captain of the guard, an Egyptian, bought him from the Ish'maelites who had brought him down there. The LORD was with Joseph, and he became a successful man; and he was in the house of his master the Egyptian, and his master saw that the LORD was with him, and that the LORD caused all that he did to prosper.

Now Joseph was handsome and good-looking. And after a time his master's wife cast her eyes upon Joseph. And although she spoke to Joseph day after day, he would not listen to her or be with her. He said to his master's wife, "Lo, my master has put everything that he has in my hand; nor has he kept back anything from me except yourself, because you are his wife; how then can I do this great wickedness, and sin against God?" But one day, when he went into the house to do his work she caught him by his garment. But he left his garment in her hand, and fled and got out of the house. When his master came home, she told him, "The Hebrew servant, whom you have brought among us, came in to me to insult me; but as soon as I lifted up my voice and cried, he left his garment with me, and fled out of the house."

When his master heard the words which his wife spoke to him, his anger was kindled. And Joseph's master took him and put him where the king's prisoners were confined, and he was there in prison. But the LORD was with Joseph and showed him steadfast love.

Some time after this, the butler of the king of Egypt and his baker offended their lord the king of Egypt, and he put them in the prison where Joseph was confined. The captain of the guard charged Joseph with them, and he waited on them. One night they both dreamed—each his own dream with its own meaning. When Joseph came to them in the morning they were troubled. So he asked, "Why are your faces downcast today?" They said to him, "We have had dreams, and there is no one to interpret them." And Joseph said to them, "Do not interpretations belong to God? Tell them to me, I pray you."

So the chief butler told his dream to Joseph, and said to him, "In my dream there was a vine before me, and on the vine there were three branches; as soon as it budded, its blossoms shot forth, and the clusters ripened into grapes. Pharaoh's cup was in my hand; and I took the grapes and pressed them into Pharaoh's cup, and placed the cup in Pharaoh's hand." Then Joseph said to him, "This is its interpretation: the three branches are three days; within three days Pharaoh will lift up your head and restore you to your office; and you shall place Pharaoh's cup in his hand as formerly, when you were his butler. But remember me, when it is well with you,

and do me the kindness, I pray you, to make mention of me to Pharaoh, and so get me out of this house. For I was indeed stolen out of the land of the Hebrews; and here also I have done nothing that they should put me into the dungeon."

From Genesis 39: 1–3, 6–12, 16–21; 40: 1, 3–15.

Joseph Becomes Governor

On Pharaoh's birthday, he made a feast for all his servants. He restored the chief butler to his butlership, and the butler placed the cup in Pharaoh's hand. Yet the chief butler did not remember Joseph, but forgot him.

After two years, Pharaoh dreamed that he was standing by the Nile, and behold, there came up out of the Nile seven cows sleek and fat, and they fed in the reed grass. And behold, seven other cows, gaunt and thin, came up out of the Nile after them, and stood by them. And the gaunt and thin cows ate up the seven sleek and fat cows. And Pharaoh awoke.

And he fell asleep and dreamed a second time; and behold, seven ears of grain, plump and good, were growing on one stalk. And behold, after them sprouted seven ears, thin and blighted by the east wind. And the thin

ears swallowed up the seven plump and full ears. And
Pharaoh awoke, and behold, it was a dream.

So in the morning his spirit was troubled; and he sent
and called for all the magicians of Egypt and all its wise
men; and Pharaoh told them his dream, but there was
none who could interpret it.

Then the chief butler said to Pharaoh, "I remember my
faults today. When Pharaoh was angry with his servants,
and put me and the chief baker in custody in the house
of the captain of the guard, we dreamed on the same
night, he and I, each having a dream with its own meaning. A young Hebrew was there with us, a servant of the
captain of the guard; and he interpreted our dreams to
us. And as he interpreted to us, so it came to pass."

Then Pharaoh sent and called Joseph, and they
brought him hastily out of the dungeon; and when he
had shaved himself and changed his clothes, he came in
before Pharaoh. And Pharaoh said to Joseph, "I have had
a dream, and there is no one who can interpret it; and I
have heard it said of you that when you hear a dream
you can interpret it." Joseph answered Pharaoh, "It is
not in me; God will give Pharaoh a favorable answer."

Then Pharaoh told Joseph his dream, and Joseph said to Pharaoh, "The seven good cows are seven years, and the seven good ears are seven years; the dream is one. The seven lean and gaunt cows that came up after them are seven years, and the seven empty ears blighted by the east wind are also seven years of famine. God has shown to Pharaoh what he is about to do. There will come seven years of great plenty throughout all the land of Egypt, but after them there will arise seven years of famine, and all the plenty will be forgotten in the land of Egypt; the famine will consume the land, and the plenty will be unknown in the land by reason of that famine which will follow, for it will be very grievous. Now therefore let Pharaoh select a man discreet and wise, and set him over the land of Egypt. Let Pharaoh proceed to appoint overseers over the land, and take the fifth part of all the food of these good years that are coming, and lay up grain under the authority of Pharaoh for food in the cities. That food shall be a reserve for the land against the seven years of famine which are to befall the land of Egypt, so that the land may not perish."

This proposal seemed good to Pharaoh and to all his servants. So Pharaoh said to Joseph, "Since God has shown you all this, there is none so discreet and wise as you are; you shall be over my house, and all my people shall order themselves as you command; only as regards the throne will I be greater than you." And Pharaoh said to Joseph, "Behold, I have set you over all the land of Egypt." And Joseph went out from the presence of Pharaoh. During the seven plenteous years he gathered up food and he stored up in every city the food from the fields around it.

The seven years of plenty that prevailed in the land of Egypt came to an end; and the seven years of famine began, as Joseph had said. The people cried to Pharaoh for bread; and Pharaoh said to all the Egyptians, "Go to Joseph; what he says to you, do." So Joseph opened all the storehouses, and sold to the Egyptians, for the famine was severe in the land of Egypt. Moreover, all the earth came to Egypt to Joseph to buy grain, because the famine was severe over all the earth.

From Genesis 40: 20–21, 23; 41: 1–17, 25–31, 33–37, 39–41, 46–48, 53–57.

Jacob Sends His Sons to Egypt

When Jacob in Israel learned that there was grain in Egypt, he said to his sons, "Go and buy grain for us there, that we may live, and not die." So ten of Joseph's brothers went down to buy grain in Egypt. But Jacob did not send Benjamin, Joseph's youngest brother, with his brothers, for he feared that harm might befall him.

Now Joseph was governor over the land; he it was who sold to all the people of the land. And Joseph's brothers came, and bowed themselves before him with their faces to the ground. Joseph saw his brothers, and knew them, but he treated them like strangers and spoke roughly to them. "Where do you come from?" he said. They said, "From the land of Canaan, to buy food." Thus Joseph knew his brothers, but they did not know him. And Joseph remembered the dreams which he had dreamed of them; and he said to them, "You are spies, you have come to see the weakness of the land." They said to him, "No, my lord, but to buy food have your servants come. We are honest men, your servants are not spies. We are twelve brothers, the sons of one man in the land of Canaan; and behold, the youngest is this day with our father, and one is no more."

Joseph said to them, "If you are honest men, let one of your brothers remain confined in prison, and let the rest go and carry grain for the famine of your households, and bring your youngest brother to me; so your words will be verified." Then they said to one another, "In truth we are guilty concerning our brother, in that we saw the distress of his soul, when he besought us and we would not listen; therefore is this distress come upon us." They did not know that Joseph understood them, for there was an interpreter between them. Then he turned away from them and wept; and he returned to them and spoke to them. And he took Simeon from them and bound him before their eyes. And Joseph gave orders to fill their

32

bags with grain, and to replace every man's money in his sack, and to give them provisions for the journey. This was done for them. Then they loaded their asses with their grain, and departed.

When they came to Jacob their father in the land of Canaan, they told him all that had befallen them. As they emptied their sacks, behold, every man's bundle of money was in his sack; and when they and their father saw their bundles of money, they were dismayed.

Now the famine was severe in the land. And when they had eaten the grain which they had brought from Egypt, their father said to them, "Go again, buy us a little food." But Judah said to him, "The man solemnly warned us, saying, 'You shall not see my face, unless your brother is with you.' If you will send our brother with us, we will go down and buy you food; but if you will not send him, we will not go down, for the man said to us, 'You shall not see my face, unless your brother is with you.'" And Judah said to Israel his father, "Send the lad with me, and we will go, that we may live and not die, both we and you and also our little ones. I will be surety for him."

Then their father Israel said to them, "If it must be so,

then do this: Take double the money with you; carry back with you the money that was returned in the mouth of your sacks; perhaps it was an oversight. Take your brother, and go to the man; may God Almighty grant you mercy before the man, that he may send back your other brother and Benjamin." So the men went down to Egypt, and stood before Joseph.

From Genesis 42: 1–4, 6–11, 13, 18–21, 23–26, 29, 35; 43: 1–5, 8–9, 11–15.

Joseph's Family Moves to Egypt

When Joseph saw Benjamin with them, he said to the steward of his house, "Bring the men into the house, for they are to dine with me at noon."

Joseph said, "Is your father well, the old man of whom you spoke?" They said, "Your servant our father is well." And he lifted up his eyes, and saw his brother Benjamin and said, "Is this your youngest brother, of whom you spoke to me? God be gracious to you, my son!"

Then Joseph could not control himself before all those who stood by him; and he cried, "Make every one go out from me." And Joseph said to his brothers, "I am Joseph; is my father still alive?" But his brothers could not answer him, for they were dismayed at his presence.

So Joseph said to his brothers, "Come near to me." And they came near. And he said, "I am your brother, Joseph, whom you sold into Egypt. And now do not be distressed, or angry with yourselves, because you sold me here; for God sent me before you to preserve for you a remnant on earth, and to keep alive for you many survivors. So it was not you who sent me here, but God. Make haste and go to my father and say to him, 'Thus says your son Joseph, God has made me lord of all Egypt; come to me, do not tarry. You shall dwell in the land of Goshen, and you shall be near me, you and your children and your children's children, and your flocks, your herds, and all that you have; and there I will provide for you, for there are yet five years of famine to come.' And now your eyes see, and the eyes of my brother Benjamin see, that it is my mouth that speaks to you." And he kissed all his brothers; and after that his brothers talked with him.

When the report was heard in Pharaoh's house, "Joseph's brothers have come," it pleased Pharaoh and his servants well. And Pharaoh said to Joseph, "Say to your brothers, 'Do this: load your beasts and go back to the land of Canaan; and take your father and your households, and come to me, and I will give you the best of the land of Egypt, and you shall eat the fat of the land.' "

So they went out of Egypt, and came to the land of Canaan to their father Jacob. And they told him, "Joseph is still alive, and he is ruler over all the land of Egypt." And his heart fainted, for he did not believe them. But when they told him all the words of Joseph, and when he saw the wagons which Joseph had sent, the spirit of their father revived; and he said, "It is enough; Joseph my son is still alive; I will go and see him before I die."

Then Joseph made ready his chariot and went up to meet his father in Goshen; and he presented himself to him, and wept.

Then Joseph settled his father and his brothers, and gave them a possession in the land of Egypt, in the best of the land, in the land of Ram'eses, as Pharaoh had commanded. And Joseph provided his father, his brothers, and all his father's household with food.

From Genesis 43: 16, 26–29; 45: 1, 3–5, 7–12, 15–18, 25–28; 46: 29; 47: 11–12.

Moses and His People

Joseph died, and all his brothers, and all that generation. But the descendants of Israel multiplied and grew exceedingly strong; so that the land was filled with them.

Now there arose a new king over Egypt, who did not know Joseph. And he said to his people, "Behold, the people of Israel are too many and too mighty for us. Come, let us deal shrewdly with them, lest they multiply, and, if war befall us, they join our enemies and fight against us and escape from the land." Therefore they set taskmasters over them to afflict them with heavy burdens; and they built for Pharaoh store cities, Pithom and Ra-am'ses. But the more they were oppressed, the more they multiplied and the more they spread abroad. And the Egyptians were in dread of the people of Israel. So they made the people of Israel serve with rigor, and made their lives bitter with hard service, in mortar and brick, and in all kinds of work in the field.

Then Pharaoh commanded all his people, "Every son that is born to the Hebrews you shall cast into the Nile, but you shall let every daughter live."

Now a man from the house of Levi went and took to wife a daughter of Levi. The woman conceived and bore a son; and when she saw that he was a goodly child, she hid him three months. And when she could hide him no longer she took a basket made of bulrushes, and daubed it with bitumen and pitch. She put the child in it and placed it among the reeds at the river's brink. And his sister stood at a distance, to know what would be done to him.

Now the daughter of Pharaoh came down to bathe at the river, and her maidens walked beside the river; she saw the basket among the reeds and sent her maid to fetch it. When she opened it she saw the child; and lo, the babe was crying. She took pity on him and said, "This is one of the Hebrews' children." Then his sister said to Pharaoh's daughter, "Shall I go and call you a nurse from the Hebrew women to nurse the child for you?" And Pharaoh's daughter said to her, "Go." So the girl went and called the child's mother. And Pharaoh's daughter said to her, "Take this child away, and nurse him for me, and I will give you your wages." So the woman took the child and nursed him. And the child grew, and she brought him to Pharaoh's daughter, and he became her son; and she named him Moses, for she said, "Because I drew him out of the water."

From Exodus 1: 6–14, 22; 2: 1–10.

The Call of Moses

One day, when Moses had grown up, he went out to his people and looked on their burdens; and he saw an Egyptian beating a Hebrew, one of his people. He looked this way and that, and seeing no one he killed the Egyp-

tian and hid him in the sand. When he went out the next day, behold, two Hebrews were struggling together; and he said to the man that did the wrong, "Why do you strike your fellow?" He answered, "Who made you a prince and a judge over us? Do you mean to kill me as you killed the Egyptian?" Then Moses was afraid, and thought, "Surely the thing is known." When Pharaoh heard of it, he sought to kill Moses. But Moses fled from Pharaoh, and stayed in the land of Mid'ian. Now the priest of Mid'ian had seven daughters and he gave Moses his daughter Zipporah to be his wife.

The people of Israel groaned under their bondage, and cried out for help, and their cry under bondage came up to God. And God heard their groaning, and God remembered his covenant with Abraham, with Isaac, and with Jacob.

Now Moses was keeping the flock of his father-in-law, Jethro, the priest of Mid'ian; and he led his flock to the west side of the wilderness, and came to Horeb, the mountain of God. And the angel of the LORD appeared to him in a flame of fire out of the midst of a bush; and he looked, and lo, the bush was burning, yet it was not consumed. God called to him out of the bush, "Moses, Moses!" And he said, "Here am I." Then he said, "Do not come near; put off your shoes from your feet, for the

place on which you are standing is holy ground." And he
said, "I am the God of your father, the God of Abraham,
the God of Isaac, and the God of Jacob." And Moses hid
his face, for he was afraid to look at God.

Then the LORD said, "I have seen the affliction of my
people who are in Egypt, and have heard their cry because of their taskmasters; I know their sufferings, and
I have come down to deliver them out of the hand of
the Egyptians, and to bring them up out of that land to
a good and broad land, a land flowing with milk and
honey. Come, I will send you to Pharaoh that you may
bring forth my people, the sons of Israel, out of Egypt."

Moses said to God, "Who am I that I should go to
Pharaoh, and bring the sons of Israel out of Egypt?" He
said, "But I will be with you; and this shall be the sign for
you, that I have sent you: when you have brought forth
the people out of Egypt, you shall serve God upon this
mountain."

But Moses said to the LORD, "I am not eloquent, but
I am slow of speech and of tongue." Then the LORD said
to him, "I will be with you." But Moses said, "Oh, LORD,
send some other person." Then the LORD said, "Is there
not Aaron, your brother, the Levite? I know that he can
speak well; he shall speak for you."

From Exodus 2: 11–16, 21–24; 3: 1–2, 4–8, 10–12; 4: 10–14, 16.

39

"Let My People Go"

The LORD said to Aaron, "Go into the wilderness to meet Moses." So he went, and met him at the mountain of God and kissed him. And Moses told Aaron all the words of the LORD with which he had sent him. Then Moses and Aaron went to Egypt and gathered together all the elders of the people of Israel. And Aaron spoke all the words which the LORD had spoken to Moses. And when they heard that the LORD had seen their affliction, they bowed their heads and worshiped.

Afterward Moses and Aaron went to Pharaoh and said, "Thus says the LORD, the God of Israel, 'Let my people go, that they may hold a feast to me in the wilderness.'" But Pharaoh said, "Who is the LORD, that I should heed his voice and let Israel go? I do not know the LORD, and moreover I will not let Israel go. Why do you take the people away from their work? Get to your burdens."

The same day Pharaoh commanded the taskmasters of the people and their foremen, "You shall no longer give the people straw to make bricks, as heretofore; let them go and gather straw for themselves. But the number of bricks which they made heretofore you shall lay upon them, you shall by no means lessen it; for they are idle; therefore they cry, 'Let us go and offer sacrifice to our God.' Let heavier work be laid upon the men that they may labor at it and pay no regard to lying words."

And the foremen of the people of Israel, whom Pharaoh's taskmasters had set over them, were beaten, and were asked, "Why have you not done all your task of making bricks today, as hitherto?" The foremen of the people of Israel met Moses and Aaron, who were waiting for them, as they came forth from Pharaoh; and they said

to them, "The Lord look upon you and judge, because you have made us offensive in the sight of Pharaoh and his servants, and put a sword in their hand to kill us."

Then Moses turned again to the Lord and said, "O Lord, why hast thou done evil to this people? Why didst thou ever send me? For since I came to Pharaoh to speak in thy name, he has done evil to this people, and thou hast not delivered thy people at all." But the Lord said to Moses, "Now you shall see what I will do to Pharaoh; for with a strong hand he will send them out, yea, with a strong hand he will drive them out of his land."

From Exodus 4: 27–31; 5: 1–2, 4, 6–9, 14, 19–23; 6: 1.

The King Is Stubborn

Then the Lord said to Moses, "Go to Pharaoh in the morning, as he is going out to the water; wait for him by the river's brink. And you shall say to him, 'The Lord, the God of the Hebrews, sent me to you, saying, "Let my people go, that they may serve me in the wilderness; and behold, you have not yet obeyed." Thus says the Lord, "By this you shall know that I am the Lord: I will strike the water in the Nile and it shall be turned to blood." ' " Moses and Aaron did as the Lord commanded.

Pharaoh turned and went into his house, and he did not lay this to heart. And all the Egyptians dug round about the Nile for water to drink, for they could not drink the water of the Nile.

Then the Lord said to Moses, "Go in to Pharaoh and say to him, 'Thus says the Lord, "Let my people go, that they may serve me. But if you refuse to let them go, behold, I will plague all your country with frogs." ' " And the frogs came up and covered the land.

Then the LORD said to Moses, "Say to Aaron, 'Strike the dust of the earth, that it may become gnats throughout all the land of Egypt.'" And they did so; Aaron struck the dust of the earth, and there came gnats on man and beast.

Then the LORD said to Moses, "Say to Pharaoh, 'Thus says the LORD, "If you will not let my people go, behold, I will send swarms of flies on you and your servants and your people, and into your houses."'" And the land was ruined by reason of the flies.

Then Pharaoh called Moses and Aaron, and said, "I will let you go to sacrifice to the LORD your God in the wilderness; only you shall not go very far away. Make entreaty for me." Then Moses said, "I will pray to the LORD that the swarms of flies may depart from Pharaoh, from his servants, and from his people, tomorrow; only let not Pharaoh deal falsely by not letting the people go to sacrifice to the LORD." And the LORD did as Moses asked, and removed the swarms of flies. But Pharaoh did not let the people go.

Then the LORD said to Moses, "Go to Pharaoh, and say, 'Thus says the LORD, the God of the Hebrews, "Let my people go, that they may serve me. For if you refuse to let them go, behold, the hand of the LORD will fall with a very severe plague upon your cattle which are in the field, the horses, the asses, the camels, the herds, and the flocks."'" And all the cattle of the Egyptians died.

And the LORD said to Moses and Aaron, "Take handfuls of ashes and throw them toward heaven. And it shall become boils on man and beast." And boils were upon all the Egyptians.

Then the LORD said to Moses, "Stand before Pharaoh, and say, 'Thus says the LORD, the God of the Hebrews,

"You are still exalting yourself against my people, and will not let them go. Behold, tomorrow about this time I will cause very heavy hail to fall, such as never has been in Egypt from the day it was founded until now." ' " And the hail struck down every plant, and shattered every tree of the field.

Then Moses and Aaron went in to Pharaoh, and said to him, "Thus says the LORD, the God of the Hebrews, 'How long will you refuse to humble yourself before me? Let my people go, that they may serve me. For if you refuse to let my people go, behold, tomorrow I will bring locusts into your country.' " And the locusts came and ate all the plants in the land and all the fruit of the trees which the hail had left; not a green thing remained.

Then the LORD said to Moses, "Stretch out your hand toward heaven that there may be darkness over the land of Egypt, a darkness to be felt." So Moses stretched out his hand toward heaven, and there was thick darkness in all the land of Egypt three days; they did not see one another, nor did any rise from his place for three days.

Moses and Aaron did all these wonders before Pharaoh; but he did not let the people of Israel go out of his land. And Moses said, "Thus says the LORD, 'Yet one plague more I will bring upon Pharaoh and upon Egypt. About midnight I will go forth in the midst of Egypt; and all the first-born in the land of Egypt shall die, from the first-born of Pharaoh who sits upon his throne, even to the first-born of the maidservant who is behind the mill; and all the first-born of the cattle.' "

From Exodus 7: 14–17, 20, 23–24; 8: 1–2, 6, 16–17, 20–21, 24–25, 28–29, 31–32; 9: 1–3, 6, 8–9, 11, 13, 17–18, 25; 10: 3–4, 14–15, 21–23; 11: 10, 4, 1, 5.

The Passover

The Lord said to Moses and Aaron, "Tell all the congregation of Israel that they shall take every man a lamb for a household, and shall keep it until the fourteenth day of this month, when they shall kill their lambs in the evening. Then they shall take some of the blood, and put it on the two doorposts and the lintel of the houses in which they eat them. They shall eat the flesh that night, roasted; with unleavened bread and bitter herbs they shall eat it. It is the Lord's passover. For I will pass through the land of Egypt that night, and I will smite all the first-born in the land of Egypt. The blood shall be a sign for you, upon the houses where you are; and when I see the blood, I will pass over you, and no plague shall fall upon you to destroy you. This day you shall keep as a feast to the Lord for ever."

Then the people of Israel did as the Lord commanded.

At midnight the Lord smote all the first-born in the land of Egypt, from the first-born of Pharaoh who sat on his throne to the first-born of the captive who was in the dungeon, and all the first-born of the cattle. And Pharaoh rose up in the night, he, and all his servants, and all the Egyptians; and there was a great cry in Egypt, for there was not a house where one was not dead. And he summoned Moses and Aaron by night, and said, "Rise up, go forth from among my people, both you and the people of Israel; and go, serve the Lord, as you have said. Take your flocks and your herds, and be gone and bless me."

From Exodus 12: 1, 3, 6–8, 11–14, 28–32.

Journey Through the Wilderness

And on that very day the LORD brought the people of Israel out of the land of Egypt; and he led the people round by the way of the wilderness toward the Red Sea. And the LORD went before them by day in a pillar of cloud to lead them along the way, and by night in a pillar of fire to give them light, that they might travel by day and by night; the pillar of cloud by day and the pillar of fire by night did not depart from before the people.

Then Moses led Israel onward from the Red Sea, and they went into the wilderness of Shur; they went three days in the wilderness and found no water. When they came to Marah, they could not drink the water because it was bitter. And the people murmured against Moses, saying, "What shall we drink?" And he cried to the LORD; and the LORD showed him a tree, and he threw it into the water, and the water became sweet.

Then they came to Elim, where there were springs and palm trees; and they encamped there.

They set out from Elim, and all the people of Israel came to the wilderness of Sin, between Elim and Sinai, on the fifteenth day of the second month after they had departed from the land of Egypt. And the whole congregation of Israel murmured against Moses and Aaron in the wilderness, and said to them, "Would that we had died by the hand of the LORD in the land of Egypt, when we sat by the fleshpots and ate bread to the full; for you

46

have brought us out into this wilderness to kill this whole assembly with hunger."

And the LORD said to Moses, "I have heard the murmurings of the people; say to them, 'At twilight you shall eat flesh, and in the morning you shall be filled with bread; you shall know that I am the LORD your God.'"

In the evening quails came up and covered the camp: and in the morning dew lay round about the camp. And when the dew had gone up, there was a fine, flake-like thing, fine as hoarfrost on the ground. When the people saw it, they said to one another, "What is it?" And Moses said to them, "It is the bread which the LORD has given you to eat."

Jethro, Moses' father-in-law, came with his sons and his wife to Moses in the wilderness where he was encamped at the mountain of God. Moses sat to judge the people, and the people stood about Moses from morning till evening. When Moses' father-in-law saw all that he was doing for the people, he said, "Why do you sit alone, and all the people stand about you from morning till evening?" And Moses said, "Because the people come to me to inquire of God; when they have a dispute, they come to me and I decide between a man and his neighbor, and I make them know the statutes of God and his decisions." Moses' father-in-law said to him, "What you are doing is not good. You and the people with you will wear yourselves out, for the thing is too heavy for you.

Choose able men from all the people, such as fear God, men who are trustworthy and who hate a bribe; and place such men over the people. And let them judge the people at all times; every great matter they shall bring to you, but any small matter they shall decide themselves."

So Moses chose able men out of all Israel, and they judged the people at all times.

From Exodus 12: 51; 13: 18, 21–22; 15: 22–25, 27; 16: 1–3, 11–15; 18: 5, 13–18, 21–22, 24–26.

The Ten Commandments

On the third new moon after the people of Israel had gone forth out of the land of Egypt, on that day they came into the wilderness of Sinai, and there Israel encamped before the mountain. And Moses went up to God, and the LORD called him out of the mountain, saying, "Thus you shall say to the people of Israel: You have seen what I did to the Egyptians, and how I bore you on eagles' wings and brought you to myself. Now therefore, if you will obey my voice and keep my covenant, you shall be my own possession among all peoples; for all the earth is mine, and you shall be to me a kingdom of priests and a holy nation."

And God spoke all these words, saying,

"I am the LORD your God, who brought you out of the land of Egypt, out of the house of bondage.

"You shall have no other gods before me.

"You shall not make yourself a graven image, or any likeness of anything that is in heaven above, or that is in the earth beneath, or that is in the water under the earth; you shall not bow down to them or serve them; for I the LORD your God am a jealous God, visiting the iniquity of the fathers upon the children to the third and the fourth

generation of those who hate me, but showing steadfast love to thousands of those who love me and keep my commandments.

"You shall not take the name of the LORD your God in vain; for the LORD will not hold him guiltless who takes his name in vain.

"Remember the sabbath day, to keep it holy. Six days you shall labor, and do all your work; but the seventh day is a sabbath to the LORD your God; in it you shall not do any work, you, or your son, or your daughter, your manservant, or your maidservant, or your cattle, or the sojourner who is within your gates; for in six days the LORD made heaven and earth, the sea, and all that is in them, and rested the seventh day; therefore the LORD blessed the sabbath day and hallowed it.

"Honor your father and your mother, that your days may be long in the land which the LORD your God gives you.

"You shall not kill.

"You shall not commit adultery.

"You shall not steal.

"You shall not bear false witness against your neighbor.

"You shall not covet your neighbor's house; you shall not covet your neighbor's wife, or his manservant, or his maidservant, or his ox, or his ass, or anything that is your neighbor's."

Moses came and told the people all the words of the LORD; and all the people answered with one voice, and said, "All the words which the LORD has spoken we will do." And Moses wrote all the words of the LORD.

From Exodus 19: 1–6; 20: 1–17; 24: 3–4.

Building the Tabernacle

The LORD said to Moses, "Speak to the people of Israel, that they take for me an offering; from every man whose heart makes him willing you shall receive the offering for me. And let them make me a sanctuary, that I may dwell in their midst.

"They shall make an ark of acacia wood; and you shall overlay it with pure gold. And you shall cast four rings of gold for it, two rings on the one side of it, and two rings on the other side of it. You shall make poles of acacia wood, and overlay them with gold. And you shall put the poles into the rings on the sides of the ark, to carry the ark by them. And you shall put into the ark the testimony which I shall give you. Then you shall make a mercy seat of pure gold; and you shall put the mercy seat on top of the ark in the most holy place.

"Moreover you shall make a tabernacle with ten curtains of fine twined linen and blue and purple and scarlet stuff; with cherubim skilfully worked.

"You shall make the altar of acacia wood.

"There I will meet with the people of Israel, and it shall be sanctified by my glory; I will consecrate the tent of meeting and the altar; Aaron also and his sons I will consecrate, to serve me as priests. And I will dwell among the people of Israel, and will be their God."

Moses said to the people of Israel, "This is the thing which the LORD has commanded. Take from among you an offering to the LORD; whoever is of a generous heart, let him bring the LORD's offering."

And Moses called every able man in whose mind the LORD had put ability, every one whose heart stirred him up to come to do the work; and they received from Moses all the freewill offering which the people of Israel had brought for doing the work on the sanctuary.

Thus all the work of the tabernacle was finished. And Moses saw all the work; as the LORD had commanded, so had they done it. And Moses blessed them.

Then the cloud covered the tent of meeting, and the glory of the LORD filled the tabernacle. Throughout all their journeys, whenever the cloud was taken up from over the tabernacle, the people of Israel would go onward; but if the cloud was not taken up, then they did not go onward. For throughout all their journeys the cloud of the LORD was upon the tabernacle by day, and fire was in it by night, in the sight of all the house of Israel.

From Exodus 25: 1–2, 8, 10–14, 16–17, 21; 26: 1, 34; 27: 1; 29: 43-45; 35: 4–5; 36: 2–3; 39: 32, 43; 40: 34, 36–38.

The People Rebel Against God

In the second year, in the second month, on the twentieth day of the month, the cloud was taken up from over the tabernacle of the testimony, and the people of Israel set out by stages from the wilderness of Sinai.

The LORD said to Moses, "Send men to spy out the land of Canaan, which I give to the people of Israel; from each tribe of their fathers shall you send a man, every one a leader." So Moses sent them according to the command of the LORD, to spy out the land of Canaan, and said to them, "Go up into the Negeb yonder, and go up into the hill country, and see what the land is, and whether the people who dwell in it are strong or weak. Be of good courage, and bring some of the fruit of the land."

At the end of forty days they returned from spying out the land. And they came to Moses and told him, "We came to the land to which you sent us; it flows with milk and honey, and this is its fruit. Yet the people in the land are strong, and the cities are fortified and very large."

Caleb said, "Let us go up at once, and occupy it; for we are well able to overcome it." Then the men who had gone up with him said, "We are not able to go up against the people; for they are stronger than we. All the people that we saw are men of great stature, and we seemed to ourselves like grasshoppers, and so we seemed to them."

Then all the congregation raised a loud cry, "Why does the LORD bring us into this land, to fall by the sword? Would it not be better for us to go back to Egypt?"

They said to one another, "Let us choose a captain, and go back to Egypt." But Joshua and Caleb, who had spied out the land, said to the people of Israel, "The

53

land which we passed through is an exceedingly good land. If the LORD delights in us, he will bring us into this land and give it to us. Only, do not rebel against the LORD; and do not fear the people of the land. The LORD is with us; do not fear them." But all the congregation said to stone Joshua and Caleb.

Then the glory of the LORD appeared at the tent of meeting to all the people of Israel.

And the LORD said to Moses and Aaron, "I have heard the murmurings of the people of Israel. Say to them, 'Of all your number, from twenty years old and upward, who have murmured against me, not one shall come into the land except Caleb and Joshua. But your little ones I will bring in, and they shall know the land which you have despised.'"

From Numbers 10: 11–12; 13: 1–3, 17–18, 20, 25–28, 30–33; 14: 1, 3–4, 6–10, 26–31.

"Remember the LORD Your God"

These words Moses spoke to all Israel beyond the Jordan in the wilderness. "The LORD your God knows your going through this great wilderness; these forty years he has been with you.

"Hear, O Israel: The LORD our God is one LORD; and you shall love the LORD your God with all your heart, and with all your soul, and with all your might. And these words which I command you this day shall be upon your heart; and you shall teach them diligently to your children, and shall talk of them when you sit in your house, and when you walk by the way, and when you lie down, and when you rise. And you shall bind them as a sign upon your hand, and they shall be as frontlets between your eyes. And you shall write them on the doorposts of your house and on your gates.

54

"So you shall keep the commandments of the LORD your God, by walking in his ways and by fearing him. For the LORD your God is bringing you into a good land, a land of brooks of water, of fountains and springs, a land of wheat and barley, of vines and fig trees and pomegranates, a land in which you will eat bread without scarcity, in which you will lack nothing. And you shall bless the LORD your God for the good land he has given you.

"Take heed lest you forget the LORD your God, by not keeping his commandments and his ordinances and his statutes, which I command you this day: lest, when you have eaten and are full, and have built goodly houses and live in them, and when your herds and flocks multiply, and your silver and gold is multiplied, and all that you have is multiplied, then your heart be lifted up, and you forget the LORD your God, who brought you out of the house of bondage. Beware lest you say in your heart, 'My power and the might of my hand have gotten me this wealth.' You shall remember the LORD your God, for it is he who gives you power to get wealth."

From Deuteronomy 1: 1; 2: 7; 6: 4–9; 8: 6–14, 17–18.

Moses' Last Days

So Moses continued to speak these words to all Israel. And he said to them, "I am a hundred and twenty years old this day; I am no longer able to go out and come in. The LORD has said to me, 'You shall not go over this Jordan.' The LORD your God himself will go over before you; and Joshua will go over at your head."

Then Moses summoned Joshua, and said to him in the sight of all Israel, "Be strong and of good courage; for you shall go with this people into the land which the LORD has sworn to their fathers to give them; and you

55

shall put them in possession of it. It is the Lord who goes before you; he will be with you, he will not fail you or forsake you; do not fear or be dismayed."

And Moses and Joshua went and presented themselves in the tent of meeting.

And the Lord commissioned Joshua the son of Nun and said, "Be strong and of good courage; for you shall bring the children of Israel into the land which I swore to give them: I will be with you."

And Moses went up from the plains of Moab to Mount Nebo, to the top of Pisgah, which is opposite Jericho. And the Lord showed him all the land, and said, "This is the land of which I swore to Abraham, to Isaac, and to Jacob, 'I will give it to your descendants.' I have let you see it with your eyes, but you shall not go over there." So Moses died in the land of Moab, but no man knows the place of his burial to this day. Moses was a hundred and twenty years old when he died; his eye was not dim, nor his natural force abated. And the people of Israel wept for Moses in the plains of Moab thirty days.

And there has not arisen a prophet since in Israel like Moses, whom the Lord knew face to face.

From Deuteronomy 31: 1–3, 7–8, 14, 23; 34: 1, 4–8, 10.

Crossing the Jordan

After the death of Moses, the Lord said to Joshua, "Moses my servant is dead; now therefore arise, go over this Jordan, you and all this people, into the land which I am giving to them. As I was with Moses, so I will be with you; I will not fail you or forsake you."

Early in the morning Joshua rose with all the people of Israel; and they came to the Jordan, and lodged there.

At the end of three days the officers went through the camp and commanded the people, "When you see the ark of the covenant of the LORD your God being carried by the priests, then you shall follow it, that you may know the way you shall go, for you have not passed this way before." And Joshua said to the priests, "Take up the ark of the covenant, and pass on before the people."

When the people set out from their tents, to pass over the Jordan with the priests bearing the ark of the covenant before them, and when those who bore the ark had come to the Jordan, and the feet of the priests were dipped in the brink of the water, the waters coming down from above stood and rose up in a heap far off, at Adam, the city that is beside Zar'ethan, and those flowing down toward the Salt Sea were wholly cut off; and the people passed over opposite Jericho. And the priests who bore the ark of the covenant of the LORD stood on dry ground in the midst of the Jordan, until all the nation finished passing over.

Then the LORD said to Joshua, "Take twelve men from the people, from each tribe a man, and command them, 'Take twelve stones from here out of the midst of the Jordan, from the very place where the priests' feet stood, and carry them over with you, and lay them down in the place where you lodge tonight.'"

The people came up out of the Jordan on the tenth day

of the first month, and they encamped in Gilgal on the
east border of Jericho. And those twelve stones, which
they took out of the Jordan, Joshua set up in Gilgal. And
he said to the people of Israel, "When your children ask
their fathers in time to come, 'What do these stones
mean?' then you shall let your children know, 'Israel
passed over this Jordan on dry ground.'"

From Joshua 1: 1–2, 5; 3: 1–4, 6, 14–17; 4: 1–3, 19–22.

The Fall of Jericho

When all the kings beyond the Jordan to the west
heard that the LORD had dried up the waters of the Jordan for the people of Israel until they had crossed over,
there was no longer any spirit in them.

Now Jericho was shut up because of the people of
Israel; none went out, and none came in. And the LORD
said to Joshua, "See, I have given into your hand Jericho,
with its king and mighty men of valor. You shall march
around the city, all the men of war going around the city
once. Thus shall you do for six days. And seven priests
shall bear seven trumpets of rams' horns before the ark;
and on the seventh day you shall march around the city
seven times, the priests blowing the trumpets. And when
they make a long blast with the ram's horn, then all the
people shall shout with a great shout; and the wall of the
city will fall down flat, and the people shall go up every
man straight before him."

So Joshua caused the ark of the LORD to compass the
city, going about it once; and they came into the camp,
and spent the night in the camp. And the second day they
marched around the city once, and returned into the
camp. So they did for six days.

On the seventh day they rose at dawn and marched around the city seven times. And at the seventh time, when the priests had blown the trumpets, Joshua said to the people, "Shout; for the LORD has given you the city." So the people raised a great shout, and the wall fell down flat, and they took the city.

Thus the LORD gave to Israel all the land which he swore to give to their fathers; and having taken possession of it, they settled there.

Then Joshua gathered all the tribes of Israel to Shechem, and they presented themselves before God. And Joshua said to all the people, "Fear the LORD, and serve him in sincerity and in faithfulness; put away the gods which your fathers served beyond the River, and in Egypt, and serve the LORD."

And the people said to Joshua, "The LORD our God we will serve, and his voice we will obey."

From Joshua 5: 1; 6: 1–5, 11, 14–16, 20; 21: 43; 24: 1–2, 14, 24.

59

In the Days of the Judges

The people served the LORD all the days of Joshua, and all the days of the elders who outlived Joshua, who had seen all the great work which the LORD had done for Israel. But there arose another generation after them, who did not know the LORD or the work which he had done for Israel.

And the people of Israel did what was evil in the sight of the LORD. They forsook the LORD, and they went after the gods of the peoples who were round about them.

So the anger of the LORD was kindled against Israel, and he gave them over to plunderers, and they could no longer withstand their enemies.

Then the LORD raised up judges, who saved the people of Israel out of the power of those who plundered them. Whenever the LORD raised up judges for them, the LORD was with the judge, and he saved them from the hand of their enemies all the days of the judge. But whenever the judge died, they turned back and behaved worse than their fathers; they did not drop any of their practices or their stubborn ways.

In those days there was no king in Israel; every man did what was right in his own eyes.

From Judges 2: 7, 10–12, 14, 16, 18–19; 21: 25.

The Story of Ruth

In the days when the judges ruled there was a famine in the land, and a certain man of Bethlehem in Judah went to sojourn in the country of Moab, he and his wife and his two sons. The name of the man was Elim'elech and the name of his wife Na'omi, and the names of his two sons were Mahlon and Chil'ion. But Elim'elech, the husband of Na'omi, died, and she was left with her two sons. These took Moabite wives; the name of the one was Orpah and the name of the other Ruth. They lived there about ten years; and both Mahlon and Chil'ion died, so that the woman was bereft of her two sons and her husband.

Then she started with her daughters-in-law to return from the country of Moab, for she had heard in the country of Moab that the LORD had visited his people and given them food. So she set out from the place where she was, with her two daughters-in-law, and they went on the way to return to the land of Judah. But Na'omi said to her two daughters-in-law, "Go, return each of you to her mother's house. May the LORD deal kindly with you, as you have dealt with the dead and with me. The LORD grant that you may find a home, each of you in the house of her husband!" Then she kissed them, and they lifted up their voices and wept. And they said to her, "No, we will return with you to your people." But Na'omi said, "Turn back, my daughters, why will you go with me?"

Then they lifted up their voices and wept again; and Orpah kissed her mother-in-law, but Ruth clung to her.

And she said, "See, your sister-in-law has gone back to her people and to her gods; return after your sister-in-law." But Ruth said, "Entreat me not to leave you or to return from following you; for where you go I will go, and where you lodge I will lodge; your people shall be my people, and your God my God; where you die I will die, and there will I be buried." When Na'omi saw that she was determined to go with her, she said no more.

So Na'omi returned, and Ruth the Moabitess her daughter-in-law with her. And they came to Bethlehem at the beginning of barley harvest.

Now Na'omi had a kinsman of her husband's, a man of wealth, whose name was Bo'az. And Ruth said to Na'omi, "Let me go to the field, and glean among the ears of grain after him in whose sight I shall find favor." And she said to her, "Go, my daughter." So she set forth and went and gleaned in the field after the reapers; and she happened to come to the part of the field belonging to Bo'az. And behold, Bo'az came from Bethlehem; and he said to the reapers, "The LORD be with you!" And they answered, "The LORD bless you." Then Bo'az said to his servant who was in charge of the reapers, "Whose maiden is this?" And the servant answered, "It is the maiden who came back with Na'omi from the country of Moab. She said, 'Pray, let me gather among the sheaves after the reapers.' So she came, and she has continued from early morning until now, without resting for a moment."

Then Bo'az said to Ruth, "Now, listen, my daughter, do not go to glean in another field, but keep close to my maidens. Let your eyes be upon the field which they are reaping, and go after them. Have I not charged the young men not to molest you? And when you are thirsty, go to the vessels and drink what the young men have drawn." Then she bowed to the ground, and said to him, "Why have I found favor in your eyes, that you should take notice of me, when I am a foreigner?" But Bo'az answered, "All that you have done for your mother-in-law since the death of your husband has been fully told me, and how you left your father and mother and your native land and came to a people that you did not know before. The LORD recompense you for what you have done, and a full reward be given you by the LORD, the God of Israel, under whose wings you have come to take refuge!" Then she said, "You are most gracious to me, my lord, for you have comforted me and spoken kindly to your maidservant, though I am not one of your maidservants."

And at mealtime Bo'az said to her, "Come here, and eat some bread, and dip your morsel in the wine." So she sat beside the reapers, and he passed to her parched grain; and she ate until she was satisfied, and she had some left over. When she rose to glean, Bo'az instructed his young men, saying, "Let her glean even among the sheaves, and do not reproach her. And also pull out some from the bundles for her, and leave it for her to glean."

So she gleaned in the field until evening; then she beat out what she had gleaned, and it was about an ephah of barley. And she took it up and went into the city; she showed her mother-in-law what she had gleaned, and she also brought out and gave her what food she had left over. And her mother-in-law said to her, "Where did you glean today? And where have you worked? Blessed be the man who took notice of you." So she told her mother-in-law with whom she had worked, and said, "The man's name with whom I worked today is Bo'az." And Na'omi said to her daughter-in-law, "Blessed be he by the LORD whose kindness has not forsaken the living or the dead! The man is a relative of ours, one of our nearest kin." And

Ruth said, "Besides, he said to me, 'You shall keep close by my servants, till they have finished all my harvest.'" And Na'omi said to Ruth, "It is well, my daughter, that you go out with his maidens, lest in another field you be molested." So she kept close to the maidens of Bo'az, gleaning until the end of the barley and wheat harvests; and she lived with her mother-in-law.

Then Na'omi her mother-in-law said to her, "My daughter, should I not seek a home for you, that it may be well with you? Now is not Bo'az our kinsman, with whose maidens you were? See, he is winnowing barley tonight at the threshing floor. Wash therefore and anoint yourself, and put on your best clothes and go down to the threshing floor; but do not make yourself known to the man until he has finished eating and drinking."

So she went down to the threshing floor and did just as her mother-in-law had told her. And when Ruth came to her mother-in-law, Na'omi said, "How did you fare, my daughter?" Then she told her all that the man had done for her, saying, "These six measures of barley he gave to me, for he said, 'You must not go back empty-handed to your mother-in-law.'" Na'omi replied, "Wait, my daughter, until you learn how the matter turns out, for Bo'az will not rest, but will settle the matter today."

When Bo'az went up to the gate, he took ten men of the elders of the city, and said, "Sit down here"; so they sat down. Then he said, "Na'omi, who has come back from the country of Moab, is selling the parcel of land which belonged to Elim'elech. You are witnesses this day that I have bought from the hand of Na'omi all that belonged to Elim'elech and all that belonged to Chil'ion and to Mahlon. Also Ruth the widow of Mahlon, I have bought to be my wife." Then all who were at the gate, and the elders, said, "We are witnesses."

So Bo'az took Ruth and she became his wife; and she bore a son. Then the women said to Na'omi, "Blessed be the LORD, who has not left you this day without next of kin; and may his name be renowned in Israel! He shall be to you a restorer of life and a nourisher of your old age; for your daughter-in-law who loves you, who is more to you than seven sons, has borne him." Then Na'omi took the child and laid him in her bosom, and became his nurse. They named him Obed; he was the father of Jesse, the father of David.

From Ruth 1: 1–11, 14–18, 22; 2: 1–23; 3: 1–3, 6, 16–18; 4: 1–3, 9–11, 13–17.

The Birth of Samuel

There was a certain man of the hill country of E'phraim, whose name was Elka'nah. The name of his wife was Hannah. They went up to worship and to sacrifice to the LORD of hosts at Shiloh. After they had eaten and drunk in Shiloh, Hannah rose. She was deeply distressed and prayed to the LORD, and wept bitterly because she had no children. And Hannah vowed a vow and said, "O LORD of hosts, if thou wilt remember me, and wilt give to thy maidservant a son, then I will give him to the LORD all the days of his life."

Now Eli the priest was sitting on the seat beside the doorpost of the temple of the LORD.

Hannah was speaking in her heart; only her lips moved, and her voice was not heard; therefore Eli took her to be a drunken woman. And Eli said to her, "How long will you be drunken? Put away your wine from you." But Hannah answered, "I have drunk no wine, but I have been pouring out my soul before the LORD." Then Eli answered, "Go in peace, and the God of Israel grant your petition."

Then the woman went her way and ate, and her countenance was no longer sad.

In due time Hannah conceived and bore a son, and she called his name Samuel, for she said, "I have asked him of the LORD."

When she had weaned him, she brought him to the house of the LORD at Shiloh, to Eli. And she said, "Oh, my lord! I am the woman who was standing here in your presence, praying to the LORD. For this child I prayed; and the LORD has granted my petition which I made to him. Therefore I have lent him to the LORD; as long as he lives, he is lent to the LORD."

And they worshiped the LORD there.

Then Elka'nah went home to Ramah. And Samuel ministered before the LORD, a boy girded with a linen ephod, in the presence of Eli the priest.

From 1 Samuel 1: 1–3, 9–11, 13–15, 17–18, 20, 24–28; 2: 11, 18.

The Word of the Lord to Samuel

Now the sons of Eli were worthless men; they had no regard for the Lord.

Now the boy Samuel was ministering to the Lord under Eli. And Samuel continued to grow both in stature and in favor with the Lord and with men.

At that time Eli, whose eyesight had begun to grow dim, was lying down in his own place; and Samuel was lying down within the temple of the Lord, where the ark of God was. Then the Lord called, "Samuel! Samuel!" and he said, "Here I am!" and ran to Eli, and said, "Here I am, for you called me." But Eli said, "I did not call; lie down again." So he went and lay down. And the LORD called again, "Samuel!" And Samuel arose and went to Eli, and said, "Here I am, for you called me." But he said, "I did not call, my son; lie down again."

Now the LORD called Samuel the third time. And he went to Eli, and said, "Here I am, for you called me." Then Eli perceived that the LORD was calling the boy. Therefore Eli said to Samuel, "Go, lie down; and if he calls you, you shall say, 'Speak LORD, for thy servant hears.'" So Samuel went and lay down in his place.

And the LORD came and stood forth, calling as at other times, "Samuel! Samuel!" And Samuel said, "Speak, for thy servant hears." Then the LORD said to Samuel, "Behold, I will fulfil against Eli all that I have spoken concerning his house, from beginning to end. And I tell him that I am about to punish his house for ever, for the iniquity which he knew, because his sons were blaspheming God, and he did not restrain them."

Samuel lay until morning; then he opened the doors of the house of the LORD. And Samuel was afraid to tell the vision to Eli. But Eli called Samuel and said, "Samuel, my son." And he said, "Here I am." And Eli said, "What was it that he told you? Do not hide it from me. May God do so to you and more also, if you hide anything from me of all that he told you." So Samuel told him everything and hid nothing from him. And he said, "It is the LORD; let him do what seems good to him."

And Samuel grew, and the LORD was with him. And he judged Israel all the days of his life.

From 1 Samuel 2: 12; 3: 1; 2: 26; 3: 2–6, 8–13, 15–19; 7: 15.

In the Days of the Kingdom

When Samuel became old, all the elders of Israel said to him, "Behold, you are old and your sons do not walk in your ways; now appoint for us a king to govern us like all the nations." But the thing displeased Samuel. And he prayed to the LORD. And the LORD said to Samuel, "The people have not rejected you, but they have rejected me from being king over them. Now then, hearken to their voice; only, you shall solemnly warn them, and show them the ways of the king who shall reign over them." So Samuel told all the words of the LORD to the people.

But the people refused to listen to Samuel; and they said, "No! but we will have a king over us, that we also may be like all the nations, and that our king may govern us and go out before us and fight our battles."

And the LORD said to Samuel, "Hearken to their voice, and make them a king."

From 1 Samuel 8: 1, 4–7, 9–10, 19–20, 22.

Saul Becomes King

There was a man of Benjamin whose name was Kish, a man of wealth; and he had a son whose name was Saul. There was not a man among the people of Israel more handsome than Saul; he was taller than any of them.

69

Now the asses of Kish were lost. So Kish said to Saul, "Take one of the servants and go and look for the asses." And they passed through the hill country of E'phraim and through the land of Benjamin, but did not find them.

Saul said to his servant, "Come, let us go back, lest my father cease to care about the asses and become anxious about us." But he said, "There is a man of God in this city, and all that he says comes true. Perhaps he can tell us about our journey." So they went to the city where the man of God was.

Now the day before Saul came, the LORD had revealed to Samuel: "Tomorrow I will send to you a man from the land of Benjamin, and you shall anoint him to be prince over my people Israel." When Samuel saw Saul, the LORD told him, "Here is the man who shall rule over my people!" Then Saul approached Samuel and said, "Tell me where is the house of the seer?" Samuel answered Saul, "I am the seer. Today you shall eat with me. In the morning I will tell you all that is on your mind. As for your asses that were lost, they have been found."

At the break of dawn Saul arose, and he and Samuel went out into the street. As they were going down to the outskirts of the city, Samuel said to Saul, "Tell the servant to pass on, and stop here yourself that I may make known to you the word of God."

Then Samuel took a vial of oil and poured it on Saul's head, and kissed him and said, "Has not the LORD anointed you to be prince over his people Israel? And you shall reign over the people of the LORD and you will save them from the hand of their enemies."

Now Samuel called the people together to the LORD at Mizpah, and Samuel said, "Do you see him whom the

70

LORD has chosen? There is none like him among the people." And the people shouted, "Long live the king!"

Then Samuel told the people the rights and duties of the kingship; and he wrote them in a book and laid it up before the LORD. Then Samuel sent all the people away, each one to his home.

When Saul had taken the kingship over Israel, he fought against all his enemies on every side. And he did valiantly and delivered Israel out of the hands of those who plundered them.

And the Philistines mustered to fight with Israel, troops like the sand on the seashore in multitude. Saul waited seven days but Samuel did not come and the people were scattering. So Saul himself offered the burnt offering. Then Samuel came and said, "What have you done? You have not kept the commandment of the LORD."

Then the word of the LORD came to Samuel: "I repent that I have made Saul king; for he has turned back from following me, and has not performed my commandments." Then Samuel was angry; and he cried to the LORD all night. And Samuel rose early to meet Saul in the morning, and said,

"Has the LORD as great delight in burnt offerings and
    sacrifices,
  as in obeying the voice of the LORD?
Behold, to obey is better than sacrifice."

Then Saul said to Samuel, "I have sinned; for I have transgressed the commandment of the LORD and your words, because I feared the people and obeyed their voice. Now therefore, I pray, pardon my sin, and return with me, that I may worship the LORD." And Samuel said to Saul, "I will not return with you; for you have rejected the word of the LORD, and the LORD has rejected you from being king over Israel." As Samuel turned to go away, Saul laid hold upon him and said, "I have sinned; yet honor me now before the elders of my people and before Israel, and return with me, that I may worship the LORD your God." So Samuel turned back after Saul; and Saul worshiped the LORD.

And Samuel did not see Saul again until the day of his death, but Samuel grieved over Saul.

From 1 Samuel 9: 1–6, 10, 15–20, 26–27; 10: 1, 17, 24–25; 13: 5, 8–9, 11, 13; 14: 47–48; 15: 10–12, 22, 24–27, 30–31, 35.

David Enters the King's Service

Now the Spirit of the LORD departed from Saul, and an evil spirit from the LORD tormented him. And Saul's servants said to him, "Let our lord now command your servants to seek out a man who is skilful in playing the lyre; and when the evil spirit from God is upon you, he will play it, and you will be well."

One of the young men said, "Behold, I have seen a son of Jesse the Bethlehemite, who is skilful in playing, a man of valor, a man of war, prudent in speech; and the LORD is with him." Therefore Saul sent messengers to Jesse, and said, "Send me David your son."

So David came to Saul, and entered his service. And Saul loved him greatly, and David became Saul's armor-bearer. Whenever David played the lyre, Saul was refreshed, and the evil spirit departed from him.

Then Jonathan, the son of Saul, made a covenant with David, and he loved David as his own soul. Jonathan stripped himself of the robe that was upon him, and

gave it to David, and his armor, and even his sword and his bow and his girdle.

And David went out and was successful wherever Saul sent him; so that Saul set him over the men of war. And this was good in the sight of all the people and also in the sight of Saul's servants. As they were coming home, the women came out of all the cities of Israel, singing and dancing, to meet King Saul, with timbrels, with songs of joy, and with instruments of music. And the women sang to one another as they made merry,

"Saul has slain his thousands,
And David his ten thousands."

But Saul was very angry, and this saying displeased him; he said, "They have ascribed to David ten thousands; and to me they have ascribed thousands; and what more can he have but the kingdom?" Saul was afraid of David, because the LORD was with him. But all Israel and Judah loved David.

And on the morrow an evil spirit from God rushed upon Saul, and he raved within his house, while David was playing the lyre, as he did day by day. Saul had his spear in his hand; and Saul cast the spear, for he thought, "I will pin David to the wall." But David evaded him twice.

Then David fled from Saul, and came and said to Jonathan, "What have I done? What is my guilt? And what is my sin before your father, that he seeks my life?" And he said to him, "Far from it! You shall not die. Behold, my father does nothing either great or small without disclosing it to me; and why should my father hide this from me? It is not so." But David replied, "Your father knows well that I have found favor in your eyes;

and he thinks, 'Let not Jonathan know this, lest he be grieved.' But truly, as the LORD lives and as your soul lives, there is but a step between me and death." Then said Jonathan to David, "Whatever you say, I will do for you. Go in peace, forasmuch as we have sworn both of us in the name of the LORD, saying, 'The LORD shall be between me and you, and between my descendants and your descendants, for ever.'" And he rose and departed; and Jonathan went into the city.

David was afraid because Saul came to seek his life. David was in the wilderness of Ziph at Horesh. And Jonathan, Saul's son, rose, and went to David, and said to him, "Fear not; for the hand of Saul my father shall not find you; you shall be king over Israel, and I shall be next to you; Saul my father also knows this." And the two of them made a covenant before the LORD.

From 1 Samuel 16: 14–16, 18–19, 21, 23; 18: 3–8, 12, 16, 10–11; 20: 1–4, 42; 23: 15–18.

David Spares Saul's Life

Then the Ziphites came to Saul at Gib'e-ah, saying, "Is not David hiding himself on the hill of Hachi'lah?" So Saul arose and went down to the wilderness of Ziph, with three thousand chosen men of Israel, to seek David.

David sent out spies, and learned that Saul had come.
Then David rose and came to the place where Saul had
encamped; and David saw the place where Saul lay, with
Abner the son of Ner, the commander of his army. The
army was encamped around him.

Then David said, "Who will go down with me into the
camp to Saul?" And Abi'shai said, "I will go down with
you." So David and Abi'shai went to the army by night;
and there lay Saul sleeping within the encampment, with
his spear struck in the ground at his head; and Abner
and the army lay around him. Then said Abi'shai to
David, "God has given your enemy into your hand this
day; now therefore let me pin him to the earth with one
stroke of the spear, and I will not strike him twice." But
David said to Abi'shai, "Do not destroy him; for who can
put forth his hand against the LORD's anointed, and be
guiltless?" So David took the spear and the jar of water
from Saul's head; and they went away. No man saw it,
or knew it, nor did any awake; for they were all asleep,
because a deep sleep had fallen upon them.

Then David went and stood on the top of the mountain, with a great space between them; and David called
to Abner, "Are you not a man? Who is like you in Israel?
Why then have you not kept watch over your lord the

king? Now see where the king's spear is, and the jar of water that was at his head."

Saul recognized David's voice, and said, "Is this your voice, my son David?" and David said, "It is my voice, my lord, O king. Why does my lord pursue after his servant? What have I done? What guilt is on my hands?"

Then Saul said, "I have done wrong; return, my son David, for I will no more do you harm, because my life was precious in your eyes this day; behold, I have played the fool, and have erred exceedingly." And David made answer, "Here is the spear, O king! Let one of the young men come over and fetch it. For the LORD gave you into my hand today, and I would not put forth my hand against the LORD's anointed. As your life was precious this day in my sight, so may my life be precious in the sight of the LORD, and may he deliver me out of all tribulation." Then Saul said, "Blessed be you, my son David! You will do many things and will succeed in them." So David went his way, and Saul returned to his place.

Now the Philistines fought against Israel; and the men of Israel fled before the Philistines, and fell slain on Mount Gilbo'a. And the Philistines overtook Saul and his sons; and the Philistines slew Jonathan and Abin'adab and Mal'chishu'a, the sons of Saul. The battle pressed hard upon Saul, and the archers found him; and he was badly wounded by the archers. Then Saul said to his armor-bearer, "Draw your sword, and thrust me through with it, lest these Philistines come and thrust me through, and make sport of me." But his armor-bearer would not; for he feared greatly. Therefore Saul took his own sword, and fell upon it.

From 1 Samuel 26: 1–2, 4–9, 12–18, 21–25; 31: 1–4.

David the King

After this David inquired of the LORD, "Shall I go up into any of the cities of Judah?" And the LORD said to him, "Go up." David said, "To which shall I go up?" And he said, "To Hebron." So David went up there. And the men of Judah came, and they anointed David king over the house of Judah.

Then all the tribes of Israel came to David at Hebron, and said, "Behold, we are your bone and flesh. In times past, when Saul was king over us, it was you that led out and brought in Israel; and the LORD said to you, 'You shall be shepherd of my people Israel, and you shall be prince over Israel.'"

So King David made a covenant with them at Hebron before the LORD, and they anointed David king over Israel. David was thirty years old when he began to reign, and he reigned forty years. At Hebron he reigned over Judah seven years and six months; and at Jerusalem he reigned over all Israel and Judah thirty-three years.

And they brought in the ark of God, and set it inside the tent which David had pitched for it; and they offered burnt offerings and peace offerings before God. And when David had finished offering the burnt offerings and the peace offerings, he blessed the people in the name of the LORD. He appointed certain of the Levites as ministers before the ark of the LORD, to invoke, to thank, and to praise the LORD, the God of Israel.

Then on that day, David first appointed that thanksgiving be sung to the LORD.

O give thanks to the LORD, call on his name,
    make known his deeds among the peoples!
Sing to him, sing praises to him,
    tell of all his wonderful works!
Glory in his holy name;
    let the hearts of those who seek the LORD rejoice!
Seek the LORD and his strength,
    seek his presence continually!
Remember the wonderful works that he has done,
    the wonders he wrought, the judgments he uttered,
O offspring of Abraham his servant,
    sons of Jacob, his chosen ones!
O give thanks to the LORD, for he is good;
    for his steadfast love endures for ever!

Now when the king dwelt in his house, and the LORD had given him rest from all his enemies round about, the king said to Nathan the prophet, "See now, I dwell in a house of cedar, but the ark of God dwells in a tent." And Nathan said to the king, "Go, do all that is in your heart; for the LORD is with you. Moreover the LORD declares to you that the LORD will make you a house. The LORD says to you, 'I will raise up your son after you. He shall build a house for my name, and your house and your kingdom shall be made sure for ever before me; your throne shall be established for ever.'"

So David reigned over all Israel; and David administered justice and equity to all his people.

When David's time to die drew near, he charged Solomon his son, saying, "I am about to go the way of all the earth. Be strong, and show yourself a man, and keep the commandment of the LORD your God, as it is written in the law of Moses, that the LORD may establish his word which he spoke concerning me, saying, 'If your sons take heed to their way, to walk before me in faithfulness with all their heart and with all their soul, there shall not fail you a man on the throne of Israel.'"

Then David slept with his fathers, and was buried in the city of David. And Solomon sat upon the throne of David his father; and his kingdom was firmly established.

From 2 Samuel 2: 1–2, 4; 5: 1–5; 1 Chronicles 16: 1–2, 4, 7–13, 34; 2 Samuel 7: 1–3, 11–13, 16; 8: 15; 1 Kings 2: 1–4, 10, 12.

Solomon Builds the Temple

Judah and Israel were as many as the sand by the sea; they ate and drank and were happy. Solomon ruled over all the kingdoms from the Eu-phra'tes to the land of the Philistines and to the border of Egypt; they brought tribute and served Solomon all the days of his life. And men came from all peoples to hear the wisdom of Solomon.

Now Hiram king of Tyre sent his servants to Solomon, when he heard that they had anointed him king in place of his father; for Hiram always loved David. And Solomon sent word to Hiram, "You know that David my father could not build a house for the name of the LORD

his God because of the warfare with which his enemies surrounded him. But now the LORD my God has given me rest on every side. And so I purpose to build a house for the name of the LORD my God. Now therefore command that cedars of Lebanon be cut for me; and my servants will join your servants, and I will pay such wages as you set." And Hiram sent to Solomon, saying, "I am ready to do all you desire in the matter of cedar and cypress timber."

In the four hundred and eightieth year after the people of Israel came out of the land of Egypt, in the fourth year of Solomon's reign over Israel, he began to build the house of the LORD. The house which King Solomon built for the LORD was sixty cubits long, twenty cubits wide, and thirty cubits high. The house was built with stone prepared at the quarry; so that neither hammer nor axe nor any tool of iron was heard in the temple, while it was being built. He was seven years in building it.

Then Solomon assembled the elders of Israel and all the heads of the tribes, the leaders of the fathers' houses of the people of Israel, before King Solomon in Jerusalem, to bring up the ark of the covenant of the LORD out of the city of David, which is Zion.

And all the elders of Israel came, and the priests took up the ark. And they brought up the ark of the LORD, the tent of meeting, and all the holy vessels that were in the tent. Then the priests brought the ark of the covenant of the LORD to its place, in the inner sanctuary of the house in the most holy place. And when the priests came out of the holy place, the glory of the LORD filled the house of the LORD.

From 1 Kings 4: 20–21, 34; 5: 1–6, 8; 6: 1–2, 7, 38; 8: 1, 6, 3–4, 6, 10–11.

Solomon Breaks the Covenant

Now King Solomon loved many foreign women from the nations concerning which the LORD had said to the people of Israel, "You shall not enter into marriage with them, neither shall they with you, for surely they will turn away your heart after their gods." When Solomon was old his wives turned away his heart after other gods; and his heart was not wholly true to the LORD his God, as was the heart of David his father. For Solomon did what was evil in the sight of the LORD, and built a high place for Chemosh the abomination of Moab, and for

83

Molech the abomination of the Ammonites, on the mountain east of Jerusalem. And so he did for all his foreign wives, who burned incense and sacrificed to their gods.

And the LORD was angry with Solomon, because his heart had turned away from the LORD, the God of Israel, who had appeared to him twice, and had commanded him concerning this thing, that he should not go after other gods; but he did not keep what the LORD commanded. Therefore the LORD said to Solomon, "Since this has been your mind and you have not kept my covenant and my statutes which I have commanded you, I will surely tear the kingdom from you and will give it to your servant. Yet for the sake of David your father I will not do it in your days, but I will tear it out of the hand of your son." And the time that Solomon reigned in Jerusalem over all Israel was forty years. And Solomon slept with his fathers, and was buried in the city of David his father; and Rehobo'am his son reigned in his stead.

From 1 Kings 11: 1–2, 4, 6–12, 42, 43.

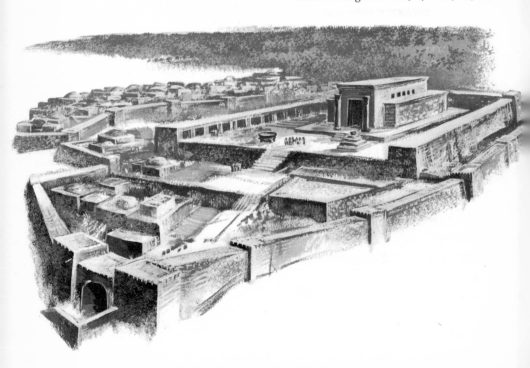

The Kingdom Is Divided

Rehobo'am went to Shechem, for all Israel had come
to Shechem to make him king. And when Jerobo'am the
son of Nebat heard of it (for he was still in Egypt,
whither he had fled from King Solomon), then Jerobo'am
returned from Egypt. And the people of Israel sent and
called him; and Jerobo'am and all the assembly of
Israel came and said to Rehobo'am, "Your father made
our yoke heavy. Now therefore lighten the hard service
of your father and his heavy yoke upon us, and we will
serve you." He said to them, "Depart for three days, then
come again to me." So the people went away.

Then King Rehobo'am took counsel with the old men,
who had stood before Solomon his father, saying, "How
do you advise me to answer this people?" And they said
to him, "If you will be a servant to this people today and
serve them, and speak good words to them, then they
will be your servants for ever." But he forsook the counsel which the old men gave him, and took counsel with
the young men who had grown up with him and he said
to them, "What do you advise that we answer this people?" And the young men said, "Thus shall you speak:

85

'I will add to your yoke. My father chastised you with whips, but I will chastise you with scorpions.' "

So Jerobo'am and all the people came to Rehobo'am the third day. And the king answered the people harshly, saying, "My father made your yoke heavy, but I will add to your yoke; my father chastised you with whips, but I will chastise you with scorpions."

And when all Israel saw that the king did not hearken to them, the people answered the king,

> "What portion have we in David?
>> We have no inheritance in the son of Jesse.
> To your tents, O Israel!
>> Look now to your own house, David."

So Israel departed to their tents. But Rehobo'am reigned over the people of Israel who dwelt in the cities of Judah.

And when all Israel heard that Jerobo'am had returned, they sent and called him to the assembly and made him king over all Israel. There was none that followed the house of David, but the tribe of Judah only.

And Rehobo'am slept with his fathers and was buried with his fathers in the city of David. And Abi'jam his son reigned in his stead.

From 1 Kings 12: 1–14, 16–17, 20; 14: 31.

The Test at Mount Carmel

Ahab began to reign over Israel, and did evil in the sight of the LORD more than all that were before him.

Now Eli'jah the Tishbite, of Tishbe in Gilead, said to Ahab, "As the LORD the God of Israel lives, before whom I stand, there shall be neither dew nor rain these years, except by my word."

After many days the word of the LORD came to Eli'jah, saying, "Go, show yourself to Ahab; and I will send rain upon the earth." When Ahab saw Eli'jah, Ahab said to him, "Is it you, you troubler of Israel?" And he answered, "I have not troubled Israel; but you have, because you have forsaken the commandments of the LORD and followed the Ba'als. Now gather all Israel at Mount Carmel, and the four hundred and fifty prophets of Ba'al."

So Ahab sent to all the people of Israel, and gathered the prophets together at Mount Carmel. And Eli'jah came near to all the people, and said, "How long will you go limping with two different opinions? If the LORD is God, follow him; but if Ba'al, then follow him." And the people did not answer him a word. Then Eli'jah said, "I, even I only, am left a prophet of the LORD; but Ba'al's prophets are four hundred and fifty men. Let two bulls be given to us; and let them choose one bull for themselves, and cut it in pieces and lay it on the wood, but put no fire to it; and I will prepare the other bull and lay it on the wood, and put no fire to it. And you call on the name of your god and I will call on the name of the LORD; and the God who answers by fire, he is God."

The people answered, "It is well spoken." Then Eli'jah said to the prophets of Ba'al, "Choose for yourselves one bull and prepare it first, for you are many; and call on the name of your god, but put no fire to it." And they took the bull, and they prepared it, and called on the name of Ba'al from morning until noon, saying, "O Ba'al, answer us!" But no one answered. And they limped about the altar which they had made. And at noon Eli'jah mocked them, saying, "Cry aloud, for he is a god; either he is musing, or he has gone aside, or he is on a journey, or perhaps he is asleep and must be awakened." And they cried aloud, and cut themselves after their custom with swords and lances, until the blood gushed out upon them. And as midday passed, they raved on until the time of the offering of the oblation, but there was no voice; no one answered, no one heeded.

Then Eli'jah repaired the altar of the LORD that had been thrown down; and he made a trench about the altar, and he put the wood in order, and cut the bull in pieces and laid it on the wood. And he said, "Fill four jars with water, and pour it on the burnt offering, and on the wood." And he said, "Do it a second time"; and they did it a second time. And he said, "Do it a third time"; and they did it a third time. And the water ran round about the altar, and filled the trench. Eli'jah came near and said, "O LORD, God of Abraham, Isaac, and Israel, let it be known this day that thou art God in Israel, and that I am thy servant, and that I have done all these things at thy word. Answer me, O LORD, answer me, that this people may know that thou, O LORD, art God."

Then the fire of the LORD fell, and consumed the burnt offering, and the wood, and the stones, and the dust, and licked up the water that was in the trench. And when all the people saw it, they fell on their faces; and they said, "The LORD, he is God; the LORD, he is God." And Eli'jah said, "Seize the prophets of Ba'al; let not one of them escape."

And Eli'jah said to Ahab, "Go up, eat and drink; for there is a sound of the rushing of rain." So Ahab went up to eat and to drink. And Eli'jah went up to the top of Carmel; and he bowed himself down upon the earth. And he said to his servant, "Go, look toward the sea."

And he went and looked, and said, "There is nothing."
And he said, "Go again seven times." And at the seventh
time he said, "Behold, a little cloud like a man's hand is
rising out of the sea." And Eli'jah said, "Go, say to Ahab,
'Prepare your chariot and go down, lest the rain stop
you.'" And in a little while the heavens grew black with
clouds, and there was a great rain. And Ahab rode and
went to Jezreel. And the hand of the LORD was on Eli'jah;
and he ran before Ahab to the entrance of Jezreel.

From 1 Kings 16: 29–30; 17: 1; 18: 1, 17–30, 32–46.

A Prophet Condemns a King

Now Naboth had a vineyard in Jezreel, beside the palace of Ahab king of Samar'ia. And Ahab said to Naboth,
"Give me your vineyard, that I may have it for a vege-
table garden, because it is near my house; and I will give
you a better vineyard for it; or I will give you its value in
money." But Naboth said, "The LORD forbid that I should
give you the inheritance of my fathers." And Ahab went

89

into his house vexed and sullen because of what Naboth had said. And he lay down on his bed, and turned away his face, and would eat no food.

But Jez'ebel his wife came to him, and said, "Why is your spirit so vexed that you eat no food?" And he said, "Because I spoke to Naboth and said to him, 'Give me your vineyard for money; or I will give you another vineyard for it'; and he answered, 'I will not give you my vineyard.'" And Jez'ebel his wife said to him, "Do you now govern Israel? Arise, and eat, and let your heart be cheerful; I will give you the vineyard of Naboth."

So she wrote letters in Ahab's name and sealed them with his seal, and she sent the letters to the elders and the nobles who dwelt with Naboth in his city. She wrote, "Proclaim a fast, and set Naboth on high among the people; and set two base fellows opposite him, and let them bring a charge against him, saying, 'You have cursed God and the king.' Then take him out, and stone him to death." And the men of his city did as Jez'ebel had sent word to them. Then they sent to Jez'ebel, saying, "Naboth has been stoned; he is dead."

As soon as Jez'ebel heard that Naboth was dead, she said to Ahab, "Arise, take possession of the vineyard of Naboth for he is not alive, but dead."

Then Ahab arose to go down to the vineyard of Naboth, to take possession of it.

And the word of the LORD came to Eli'jah, saying, "Arise, go down to meet Ahab king of Israel, who is in Samar'ia. He is in the vineyard of Naboth, where he has gone to take possession. Say to him, 'Thus says the LORD, "Have you killed, and also taken possession?"'"

Ahab said to Eli'jah, "Have you found me, O my en-

90

emy?" He answered, "I have found you, because you have sold yourself to do what is evil in the sight of the Lord. Behold, I will bring evil upon you; I will utterly sweep you away, and will cut off from Ahab every male, bond or free, in Israel. And the Lord also said, 'The dogs shall eat Jez'ebel within the bounds of Jezreel.'"

For three years Syria and Israel continued without war. And Ahab king of Israel said to Jehosh'aphat, king of Judea, "Will you go with me to battle against Syria at Ramoth-gilead?"

So Ahab the king of Israel and Jehosh'aphat the king of Judah went up to Ramoth-gilead. And the king of Israel disguised himself and went into battle.

But a certain man drew his bow at a venture, and struck the king of Israel between the scale armor and the breastplate. So Ahab the king of Israel died, and was brought to Samar'ia, and buried.

From 1 Kings 21: 1–11, 14–21, 23; 22: 1, 3–4, 29–30, 34, 37.

Amos Warns Israel

The words of Amos, who was among the shepherds of Teko'a, which he saw concerning Israel in the days of Uzzi'ah king of Judah and in the days of Jerobo'am the son of Jo'ash, king of Israel.

Hear this word that the Lord has spoken against you, O people of Israel, against the whole family which I brought up out of the land of Egypt: "You only have I known of all the families of the earth; therefore I will punish you for all your iniquities."

You hate him who reproves in the gate,
    and you abhor him who speaks the truth.

Therefore because you trample upon the poor
    and take from him exactions of wheat,
you have built houses of hewn stone,
    but you shall not dwell in them;
you have planted pleasant vineyards,
    but you shall not drink their wine.
For I know how many are your transgressions,
    and how great are your sins—
you who afflict the righteous, who take a bribe,
    and turn aside the needy in the gate.
Therefore he who is prudent will keep silent in such
    a time;
    for it is an evil time.

Then Amazi'ah the priest of Bethel sent to Jerobo'am king of Israel, saying, "Amos has conspired against you in the midst of the house of Israel."

And Amazi'ah said to Amos, "O seer, go, flee away to the land of Judah, and eat bread there, and prophesy there; but never again prophesy at Bethel, for it is the king's sanctuary, and it is a temple of the kingdom."

Then Amos answered Amazi'ah, "I am no prophet, nor a prophet's son; but I am a herdsman, and a dresser of sycamore trees, and the LORD took me from following the flock, and the LORD said to me, 'Go, prophesy to my people Israel.'

"Now therefore hear the word of the LORD."

Seek good, and not evil,
    that you may live;
and so the LORD, the God of hosts, will be with you,
    as you have said.

Hate evil, and love good,
   and establish justice in the gate;
it may be that the Lord, the God of hosts,
   will be gracious to the remnant of Joseph.
The Lord says,
"I hate, I despise your feasts,
   and I take no delight in your solemn assemblies.
Even though you offer me your burnt offerings and
      cereal offerings,
   I will not accept them,
and the peace offerings of your fatted beasts
   I will not look upon.
Take away from me the noise of your songs;
   to the melody of your harps I will not listen.
But let justice roll down like waters,
   and righteousness like an ever-flowing stream."

From Amos 1: 1; 3: 1–2; 5: 10–13; 7: 10, 12–16; 5: 14–16, 21–24.

Samaria Is Captured

Hoshe'a began to reign in Samar'ia over Israel. And he did what was evil in the sight of the Lord. Against him came up Shalmane'ser king of Assyria. He invaded all the land and came to Samar'ia, and for three years he besieged it. He captured Samar'ia, and he carried the Israelites away to Assyria.

And this was so, because the people of Israel had sinned against the Lord their God, who had brought them up out of the land of Egypt from under the hand of Pharaoh king of Egypt, and had feared other gods and walked in the customs of the nations whom the Lord drove out before the people of Israel. Yet the Lord warned Israel and Judah by every prophet and every seer, saying, "Turn from your evil ways and keep my commandments and my statutes, in accordance with all the law which I commanded your fathers, and which I sent to you by my servants the prophets." But they would not listen, but were stubborn, as their fathers had been. Therefore the LORD was very angry with Israel, and removed them out of his sight; none was left but the tribe of Judah only.

From 2 Kings 17: 1–3, 5–8, 13–14, 18.

Jerusalem Is Besieged

Hezeki'ah king of Judah, did what was right in the eyes of the LORD. Hezeki'ah trusted in the LORD the God of Israel; so that there was none like him among all the kings of Judah after him, nor among those who were before him. And the LORD was with him; wherever he went, he prospered. He rebelled against the king of Assyria, and would not serve him.

In the fourteenth year of King Hezeki'ah, Sennach'-erib king of Assyria sent the Rab'shakeh with a great army against King Hezeki'ah at Jerusalem. When they arrived, they came and stood by the conduit of the upper pool. And when they called for the king, there came out to them Eli'akim, who was over the household, and Sheb-nah the secretary, and Jo'ah the recorder.

Then the Rab'shakeh stood and called out in a loud voice in the language of Judah: "Hear the word of the great king, the king of Assyria! Thus says the king: 'Do not let Hezeki'ah deceive you, for he will not be able to deliver you out of my hand. Do not let Hezeki'ah make you to rely on the LORD.' For thus says the king of Assyria: 'Make your peace with me and come out to me;

then every one of you will eat of his own vine, and every one of his own fig tree, and every one of you will drink the water of his own cistern; until I come and take you away to a land like your own. And do not listen to Hezeki'ah when he misleads you by saying, The LORD will deliver us. Has any of the gods of the nations ever delivered his land out of the hand of the king of Assyria? Have they delivered Samar'ia out of my hand? Who among all the gods of the countries have delivered their countries out of my hand, that the LORD should deliver Jerusalem out of my hand?' "

But the people were silent and answered him not a word, for the king's command was, "Do not answer him." Then Eli'akim, who was over the household, and Shebna the secretary, and Jo'ah the recorder, came to Hezeki'ah with their clothes rent, and told him the words of the Rab'shakeh.

When King Hezeki'ah heard it, he rent his clothes, and covered himself with sackcloth, and went into the house of the LORD. And he sent Eli'akim and Shebnah and the senior priests to the prophet Isaiah.

When the servants of King Hezeki'ah came to Isaiah, Isaiah said to them, "Say to your master, 'Thus says the LORD: Do not be afraid because of the words that you have heard, with which the servants of the king of Assyria have reviled me. Behold, I will put a spirit in him, so that he shall hear a rumor and return to his own land; and I will cause him to fall by the sword.'

"Therefore thus says the LORD concerning the king of Assyria, He shall not come to this city or shoot an arrow there, or come before it with a shield or cast up a mound against it. By the way that he came, by the same he shall return, and he shall not come into this city, says the

LORD. For I will defend this city to save it, for my own
sake and for the sake of my servant David."

From 2 Kings 18: 1, 3, 5, 7, 13, 17–18, 28–37; 19: 1–2, 5–7, 32–34.

The Book of the Law Is Found

Josi'ah was eight years old when he began to reign,
and he reigned thirty-one years in Jerusalem. And he
did what was right in the eyes of the LORD.

In the eighteenth year of King Josi'ah, the king sent
Shaphan the secretary to the house of the LORD, saying,
"Go up to Hilki'ah the high priest, that he may reckon
the amount of the money which the keepers of the thresh-
old have collected from the people; and let it be given
into the hand of the workmen who have the oversight
of the house of the LORD; and let them give it to the
carpenters, and builders, and masons, as well as for buy-
ing timber and quarried stone to repair the house. But
no accounting shall be asked from them for the money,
for they deal honestly."

And Hilki'ah the high priest said to Shaphan the secretary, "I have found the book of the law in the house of
the LORD." And Hilki'ah gave the book to Shaphan, and
he read it. And Shaphan the secretary came to the king,
and read the book before the king.

And when the king heard the words of the book of the
law, he rent his clothes. And the king commanded
Hilki'ah the priest, and Shaphan the secretary, saying,
"Go, inquire of the LORD for me, and for the people, and
for all Judah, concerning the words of this book that
has been found; for great is the wrath of the LORD that
is kindled against us, because our fathers have not
obeyed the words of this book."

Then the king went up to the house of the LORD, and with him all the men of Judah, and the priests and the prophets, all the people, both small and great; and he read in their hearing all the words of the book of the covenant which had been found in the house of the LORD.

And the king stood by the pillar and made a covenant before the LORD, to walk after the LORD and to keep his commandments, with all his heart and soul, to perform the words of this covenant that were written in this book; and all the people joined in the covenant.

From 2 Kings 22: 1–13; 23: 1–3.

The Call of Jeremiah

The words of Jeremiah, to whom the word of the LORD came in the days of Josi'ah, king of Judah. It came also in the days of Jehoi'akim the son of Josi'ah, king of Judah, and until the end of the eleventh year of Zede-ki'ah, king of Judah, until the captivity of Jerusalem.

98

Now the word of the LORD came to me saying,
"Before I formed you in the womb I knew you,
   and before you were born I consecrated you;
   I appointed you a prophet to the nations."
Then I said, "Ah, Lord GOD! Behold, I do not know
how to speak, for I am only a youth."
But the LORD said to me,
"Do not say, 'I am only a youth';
   for to all to whom I send you you shall go,
   and whatever I command you you shall speak.
   Be not afraid of them,
   for I am with you to deliver you."

Then the LORD put forth his hand and touched my
mouth; and the LORD said to me, "Behold, I have put my
words in your mouth.

"Stand in the gate of the LORD's house, and proclaim
there this word, and say, Hear the word of the LORD, all
you men of Judah who enter these gates to worship the
LORD. Thus says the LORD of hosts, the God of Israel,
Amend your ways and your doings, and I will let you
dwell in this place. Do not trust in these deceptive
words: 'This is the temple of the LORD, the temple of the
LORD, the temple of the LORD.'

"For if you truly amend your ways and your doings,
if you truly execute justice one with another, if you do
not oppress the alien, the fatherless or the widow, or shed
innocent blood in this place, and if you do not go after
other gods to your own hurt, then I will let you dwell in
this land that I gave of old to your fathers for ever.

"Behold, you trust in deceptive words to no avail. Will
you steal, murder, commit adultery, swear falsely, burn
incense to Ba'al, and go after other gods that you have

not known, and then come and stand before me in this house, which is called by my name, and say, 'We are delivered!'—only to go on doing all these abominations? Has this house, which is called by my name, become a den of robbers in your eyes?"

From Jeremiah 1: 1–9; 7: 2–11.

"Thus Says the LORD"

Jeremiah stood in the court of the LORD's house, and said to all the people: "Thus says the LORD of hosts, the God of Israel, Behold, I am bringing upon this city and upon all its towns all the evil that I have pronounced against it, because they have stiffened their neck, refusing to hear my words."

Now Pashhur the priest, who was chief officer in the house of the LORD, heard Jeremiah prophesying these things. Then Pashhur beat Jeremiah the prophet, and put him in the stocks that were in the upper Benjamin Gate of the house of the LORD.

On the morrow, when Pashhur released Jeremiah from

the stocks, Jeremiah said to him, "The LORD does not call your name Pashhur, but Terror on every side. For thus says the LORD: Behold, I will make you a terror to yourself and to all your friends. They shall fall by the sword of their enemies while you look on. And I will give all Judah into the hand of the king of Babylon; he shall carry them captive to Babylon."

In the fourth year of Jehoi'akim the son of Josi'ah, king of Judah, this word came to Jeremiah from the LORD: "Take a scroll and write on it all the words that I have spoken to you against Israel and Judah and all the nations from the days of Josi'ah until today. It may be that the house of Judah will hear all the evil which I intend to do to them, so that every one may turn from his evil way, and that I may forgive their iniquity and their sin."

Then Jeremiah called Baruch, and Baruch wrote upon a scroll at the dictation of Jeremiah all the words of the LORD which he had spoken to him.

In the fifth year of Jehoi'akim the son of Josi'ah, king of Judah, in the ninth month, all the people in Jerusalem and all the people who came from the cities of Judah to Jerusalem proclaimed a fast before the LORD. Then, in the hearing of all the people, Baruch read the words of Jeremiah from the scroll, in the house of the LORD.

When Micai'ah heard all the words of the LORD from the scroll, he went down to the king's house; and all the princes were sitting there, and Micai'ah told them all the words that he had heard, when Baruch read the scroll.

So they went into the court to the king; and reported all the words to the king. Then the king sent Jehu'di to get the scroll, and Jehu'di read it to the king.

The king was sitting in the winter house and there was a fire burning in the brazier before him. As Jehu'di read three or four columns, the king would cut them off with a penknife and throw them into the fire in the brazier, until the entire scroll was consumed in the fire. Yet neither the king, nor any of his servants who heard all these words, was afraid.

And the king commanded Jerah'meel the king's son to seize Baruch the secretary and Jeremiah the prophet, but the LORD hid them.

Now, after the king had burned the scroll with the words which Baruch wrote at Jeremiah's dictation, the word of the LORD came to Jeremiah: "Take another scroll and write on it all the former words that were in the first scroll, which Jehoi'akim the king of Judah has burned."

Then Jeremiah took another scroll and gave it to Baruch, who wrote on it at the dictation of Jeremiah all the words of the scroll which Jehoi'akim king of Judah had burned in the fire; and many similar words were added to them.

From Jeremiah 19: 14–15; 20: 1–4; 36: 1–4, 9–13, 20–24, 26–28, 32.

Jeremiah Accused of Treason

Now Zedeki'ah was made king in the land of Judah. And Jeremiah was still going in and out among the people, for he had not yet been put in prison. The army of Pharaoh had come out of Egypt; and when the Chalde'ans who were besieging Jerusalem heard news of them, they withdrew from Jerusalem.

Then Jeremiah set out from Jerusalem to go to the land of Benjamin to receive his portion there among the people. When he was at the Benjamin Gate, a sentry there named Iri'jah seized Jeremiah, saying, "You are deserting to the Chalde'ans."

And Jeremiah said, "It is false; I am not deserting to the Chalde'ans."

But Iri'jah would not listen to him, and seized Jeremiah and brought him to the princes. And the princes were enraged at Jeremiah, and they beat him and imprisoned him in the house of Jonathan the secretary, for it had been made a prison.

When Jeremiah had come to the dungeon cells, and remained there many days, King Zedeki'ah sent for him, and received him. The king questioned him secretly in his house, and said, "Is there any word from the LORD?"

Jeremiah said, "There is. You shall be delivered into the hand of the king of Babylon."

Jeremiah also said to King Zedeki'ah, "What wrong have I done to you or your servants or this people, that you have put me in prison? Now hear, I pray you, O my lord the king: let my humble plea come before you, and do not send me back to the house of Jonathan the secretary, lest I die there."

So King Zedeki'ah gave orders, and they committed

Jeremiah to the court of the guard; and a loaf of bread was given him daily from the bakers' street, until all the bread of the city was gone.

Then the princes said to the king, "Let this man be put to death, for he is weakening the hands of the soldiers who are left in this city, and the hands of all the people, by speaking such words to them. For this man is not seeking the welfare of this people, but their harm."

King Zedeki'ah said, "Behold, he is in your hands; for the king can do nothing against you."

So they took Jeremiah and cast him into the cistern, which was in the court of the guard, letting Jeremiah down by ropes. And there was no water in the cistern, but only mire, and Jeremiah sank in the mire.

When E'bed-mel'ech the Ethiopian, a eunuch, who was in the king's house, heard that they had put Jeremiah into the cistern—the king was sitting in the Benjamin Gate—E'bed-mel'ech went from the king's house and said to the king, "My lord the king, these men have done evil in all that they did to Jeremiah the prophet by casting him into the cistern; and he will die there."

Then the king commanded E'bed-mel'ech, "Take three men with you from here, and lift Jeremiah the prophet out of the cistern before he dies."

So E'bed-mel'ech took the men with him and went to the house of the king, to a wardrobe of the storehouse, and took from there old rags and worn-out clothes, which he let down to Jeremiah in the cistern by ropes.

Then E'bed-mel'ech said to Jeremiah, "Put the rags and clothes between your armpits and the ropes."

Jeremiah did so. Then they drew Jeremiah up with ropes and lifted him out of the cistern. And Jeremiah remained in the court of the guard.

From Jeremiah 37: 1, 4–5, 12–18, 20–21; 38: 4–13.

Jerusalem Is Captured

Zedeki'ah reigned in Jerusalem, and he did what was evil in the sight of the LORD. And Zedeki'ah rebelled against the king of Babylon. Nebuchadnez'zar king of Babylon came with all his army against Jerusalem, and laid siege to it.

The famine was so severe in the city that there was no food for the people. Then a breach was made in the city; the king with all the men of war fled by night.

But the army pursued Zedeki'ah the king, and captured him, and brought him up to Nebuchadnez'zar, the king of Babylon, who passed sentence upon him, and bound him in fetters, and took him to Babylon.

The captain of the bodyguard, a servant of the king of Babylon, came to Jerusalem. And he burned the house of the LORD, and the king's house and all the houses of Jerusalem; every great house he burned down, and broke down the walls around Jerusalem. And the

rest of the people who were left in the city, the captain
of the guard carried into exile in Babylon. But the captain of the guard left some of the poorest of the land to
be vinedressers and plowmen.

So Judah was taken into exile out of its land.

The captain of the guard took Jeremiah and said to
him, "Now, behold, I release you today from the chains
on your hands. If it seems good to you to come with me
to Babylon, come, and I will look after you well; but if
it seems wrong to you to come with me to Babylon, do
not come. See, the whole land is before you; go wherever
you think it good and right to go. If you remain, then
return to Gedali'ah whom the king of Babylon appointed
governor of the cities of Judah, and dwell with him
among the people; or go wherever you think it right."

So the captain of the guard gave him an allowance of
food and a present, and let him go. Then Jeremiah went
to Gedali'ah and dwelt with him among the people who
were left in the land.

From 2 Kings 24: 18–20; 25: 1, 3–12, 21; Jeremiah 40: 2, 4–6.

Hope Comes from God

> How lonely sits the city
> that was full of people!
> Judah has gone into exile because of affliction
> and hard servitude;
> she dwells now among the nations,
> but finds no resting place;
> her pursuers have all overtaken her
> in the midst of her distress.

Jerusalem remembers
in the days of her affliction and bitterness
all the precious things
that were hers from days of old.

But this I call to mind,
and therefore I have hope:

The steadfast love of the LORD never ceases,
his mercies never come to an end;
they are new every morning;
great is thy faithfulness.
"The LORD is my portion," says my soul,
"therefore I will hope in him."

The LORD is good to those who wait for him,
to the soul that seeks him.
It is good that one should wait quietly
for the salvation of the LORD.

For the Lord will not
cast off for ever,
but, though he cause grief, he will have compassion
according to the abundance of his steadfast love;
for he does not willingly afflict
or grieve the sons of men.

From Lamentations 1: 1, 3, 7; 3: 21–26, 31–33.

"Behold, the days are coming, says the LORD, when I
will make a new covenant with the house of Israel and
the house of Judah, not like the covenant which I made
with their fathers when I took them by the hand to bring

them out of the land of Egypt, my covenant which they broke. But this is the covenant which I will make with the house of Israel after those days: I will put my law within them, and I will write it upon their hearts; and I will be their God, and they shall be my people. And no longer shall each man teach his neighbor and each his brother, saying, 'Know the LORD,' for they shall all know me, from the least of them to the greatest; for I will forgive their iniquity, and remember their sin no more."

From Jeremiah 31: 31–34.

The Temple Rebuilt

In the first year of Cyrus king of Persia, the LORD stirred up the spirit of Cyrus king of Persia so that he made a proclamation throughout all his kingdom:

"Thus says Cyrus king of Persia: The LORD, the God of heaven, has given me all the kingdoms of the earth, and he has charged me to build him a house at Jerusalem, which is in Judah. Whoever is among you of all his people, may his God be with him, and let him go up to Jerusalem, and rebuild the house of the LORD."

So the people of the province who came up out of the captivity returned to Jerusalem and Judah, each to his own town.

After this, in the reign of Ar-ta-xerx'es king of Persia, Ezra went up to Jerusalem from Babylonia. He was a scribe skilled in the law of Moses which the LORD the God of Israel had given; and the king granted him all that he asked, for the hand of the LORD was upon him.

For Ezra had set his heart to study the law of the LORD, and to do it, and to teach his statutes and ordinances in Israel.

From Ezra 1: 1–3; 2: 1; 7: 1, 6, 10.

The Work of Nehemiah

The words of Nehemi'ah the son of Hacali'ah.

As I was in Susa the capital, Hana'ni, one of my brethren, came with certain men out of Judah; and I asked them concerning the Jews that survived, who had escaped exile, and concerning Jerusalem. And they said, "The survivors who escaped exile are in great trouble and shame; the wall of Jerusalem is broken down, and its gates are destroyed by fire." When I heard these words I sat down and wept, and mourned for days; and I continued fasting and praying before the God of heaven.

Now I was cupbearer to King Ar-ta-xerx'es, and the king said to me, "Why is your face sad, seeing you are not sick?" Then I was very much afraid. I said to the king, "Let the king live for ever! Why should not my face be sad, when the city, the place of my father's sepulchres, lies waste, and its gates have been destroyed by fire?" Then the king said to me, "For what do you make request?" So I prayed to the God of heaven. And I said to the king, "If it pleases the king, and if your servant has found favor in your sight, send me to Judah, to the city of my fathers' sepulchres, that I may rebuild it." And the king granted me what I asked, for the good hand of my God was upon me.

So I came to Jerusalem and was there three days. Then I arose in the night, I and a few men with me. There was no beast with me but the beast on which I rode. I went out by night by the Valley Gate and I inspected the walls of Jerusalem which were broken down and its gates which had been destroyed by fire. And the officials did not know where I had gone or what I was doing.

Then I said to the Jews, "You see the trouble we are in, how Jerusalem lies in ruins with its gates burned. Come, let us build the wall of Jerusalem, that we may no longer suffer disgrace." And I told them of the hand of my God which had been upon me for good, and also of the words which the king had spoken to me. And they said, "Let us rise up and build." So they strengthened their hands for the good work. But when Sanbal'lat the Hor'-onite and Tobi'ah the Ammonite and Geshem the Arab heard of it, they derided us and despised us and said, "What is this thing that you are doing? Are you rebelling against the king?" Then I replied to them, "The God of heaven will make us prosper, and we his servants will arise and build; but you have no portion or right or memorial in Jerusalem."

Sanbal'lat was angry and greatly enraged, and he ridi-

111

culed the Jews. And he said in the presence of his brethren and of the army of Samar'ia, "What are these feeble Jews doing? Will they restore things? Will they sacrifice? Will they finish up in a day? Will they revive the stones out of the heaps of rubbish, and burned ones at that?" Tobi'ah the Ammonite was by him, and he said, "Yes, what they are building—if a fox goes up on it he will break down their stone wall!"

So we built the wall; and all the wall was joined together to half its height. For the people had a mind to work. And we prayed to our God, and set a guard as a protection day and night against Sanbal'lat, Tobi'ah and Geshem.

From that day on, half of my servants worked on construction, and half of them held the spears from the break of dawn till the stars came out. I also said to the people at that time, "Let every man and his servant pass the night within Jerusalem, that they may be a guard for us by night and may labor by day." So neither I nor my brethren nor my servants nor the men of the guard who followed me, none of us took off our clothes; each kept his weapon in his hand.

So the wall was finished in fifty-two days. And when all our enemies heard of it, all the nations round about us were afraid and fell greatly in their own esteem; for they perceived that this work had been accomplished with the help of our God.

And at the dedication of the wall of Jerusalem, the people celebrated with gladness, with thanksgivings and with singing, with cymbals, harps, and lyres. And the joy of Jerusalem was heard afar off.

From Nehemiah 1: 1–4, 11; 2: 1–5, 8, 11–13, 16–20; 4: 1–3, 6, 9, 16, 21–23; 6: 15–16; 12: 27, 43.

Psalms

The LORD is my shepherd, I shall not want;
   he makes me lie down in green pastures.
He leads me beside still waters;
   he restores my soul.
He leads me in paths of righteousness
   for his name's sake.

Even though I walk through the valley of the
     shadow of death,
   I fear no evil;
   for thou art with me;
   thy rod and thy staff,
   they comfort me.

Thou preparest a table before me
   in the presence of my enemies;
thou anointest my head with oil,
   my cup overflows.
Surely goodness and mercy shall follow me
   all the days of my life;
and I shall dwell in the house of the LORD
   for ever.

Psalms 23: 1–6.

O Lord, our Lord,
how majestic is thy name in all the earth!

When I look at thy heavens, the work of thy fingers,
the moon and the stars which thou hast established;
what is man that thou art mindful of him,
and the son of man that thou dost care for him?

Yet thou hast made him little less than God,
and dost crown him with glory and honor.
Thou hast given him dominion over the works of
thy hands;
thou hast put all things under his feet,
all sheep and oxen,
and also the beasts of the field,
the birds of the air, and the fish of the sea,
whatever passes along the paths of the sea.

O Lord, our Lord,
how majestic is thy name in all the earth!

From Psalms 8: 1, 3–9.

The heavens are telling the glory of God;
and the firmament proclaims his handiwork.
Day to day pours forth speech,
and night to night declares knowledge.
There is no speech, nor are there words;
their voice is not heard;
yet their voice goes out through all the earth,
and their words to the end of the world.

114

The law of the LORD is perfect,
   reviving the soul;
the testimony of the LORD is sure,
   making wise the simple;
the precepts of the LORD are right,
   rejoicing the heart;
the commandment of the LORD is pure,
   enlightening the eyes;
the fear of the LORD is clean,
   enduring for ever;
the ordinances of the LORD are true,
   and righteous altogether.
More to be desired are they than gold,
   even much fine gold;
sweeter also than honey
   and drippings of the honeycomb.

Moreover by them is thy servant warned;
   in keeping them there is great reward.
But who can discern his errors?
   Clear thou me from hidden faults.
Keep back thy servant also from presumptuous sins;
   let them not have dominion over me!
Then I shall be blameless,
   and innocent of great transgression.

Let the words of my mouth and the meditation of
   my heart
   be acceptable in thy sight,
   O LORD, my rock and my redeemer.

From Psalms 19: 1–4, 7–14.

The earth is the LORD's and the fulness thereof,
   the world and those who dwell therein;
for he has founded it upon the seas,
   and established it upon the rivers.

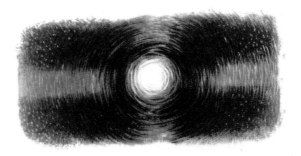

Who shall ascend the hill of the LORD?
   And who shall stand in his holy place?
He who has clean hands and a pure heart,
   who does not lift up his soul to what is false,
   and does not swear deceitfully.
He will receive blessing from the LORD,
   and vindication from the God of his salvation.
Such is the generation of those who seek him,
   who seek the face of the God of Jacob.

Lift up your heads, O gates!
  and be lifted up, O ancient doors!
  that the King of glory may come in.
Who is the King of glory?
  The LORD, strong and mighty,
  the LORD, mighty in battle!
Lift up your heads, O gates!
  and be lifted up, O ancient doors!
  that the King of glory may come in.
Who is this King of glory?
  The LORD of hosts,
  he is the King of glory!

Psalms 24: 1–10.

God is our refuge and strength,
  a very present help in trouble.
Therefore we will not fear though the earth
    should change,
  though the mountains shake in the heart of
    the sea;
though its waters roar and foam,
  though the mountains tremble with its tumult.
"Be still, and know that I am God.
  I am exalted among the nations,
  I am exalted in the earth!"
The LORD of hosts is with us;
  the God of Jacob is our refuge.

From Psalms 46: 1–3, 10–11.

Create in me a clean heart, O God,
  and put a new and right spirit within me.
Cast me not away from thy presence,
  and take not thy holy Spirit from me.
Restore to me the joy of thy salvation,
  and uphold me with a willing spirit.

Psalms 51: 10–12.

May God be gracious to us and bless us
  and make his face to shine upon us,
that thy way may be known upon earth,
  thy saving power among all nations.

Let the peoples praise thee, O God;
  let all the peoples praise thee!

Let the nations be glad and sing for joy,
   for thou dost judge the peoples with equity
   and guide the nations upon earth.

Let the peoples praise thee, O God;
   let all the peoples praise thee!

The earth has yielded its increase;
   God, our God, has blessed us.
God has blessed us;
   let all the ends of the earth fear him!

Psalms 67: 1–7.

LORD, thou hast been our dwelling place
   in all generations.
Before the mountains were brought forth,
   or ever thou hadst formed the earth and the
      world,
   from everlasting to everlasting thou art God.
For a thousand years in thy sight
      are but as yesterday when it is past,
      or as a watch in the night.
So teach us to number our days
      that we may get a heart of wisdom.
Satisfy us in the morning with thy steadfast love,
      that we may rejoice and be glad all our days.

From Psalms 90: 1–2, 4, 12, 14.

119

Make a joyful noise to the LORD, all the lands!
  Serve the LORD with gladness!
  Come into his presence with singing!

Know that the LORD is God!
  It is he that made us, and we are his;
  we are his people, and the sheep of his pasture.

Enter his gates with thanksgiving,
  and his courts with praise!
  Give thanks to him, bless his name!

For the LORD is good;
  his steadfast love endures for ever,
  and his faithfulness to all generations.

Psalms 100: 1–5.

Bless the LORD, O my soul;
   and all that is within me, bless his holy name!
Bless the LORD, O my soul,
   and forget not all his benefits,
who forgives all your iniquity,
   who heals all your diseases,
who crowns you with steadfast love and mercy,
   who satisfies you with good as long as you live.
The LORD is merciful and gracious,
   slow to anger and abounding in steadfast love.
He does not deal with us according to our sins,
   nor requite us according to our iniquities.
For as the heavens are high above the earth,
   so great is his steadfast love toward those who
      fear him;
as far as the east is from the west,
   so far does he remove our transgressions from us.

From Psalms 103: 1–5, 8, 10–12.

Bless the LORD, O my soul!
   O LORD my God, thou art very great!
Thou art clothed with honor and majesty,
   who coverest thyself with light as with a garment,
who hast stretched out the heavens like a tent,
   who hast laid the beams of thy chambers on
      the waters,
who makest the clouds thy chariot,
   who ridest on the wings of the wind,
who makest the winds thy messengers,
   fire and flame thy ministers.

Thou makest springs gush forth in the valleys;
   they flow between the hills,
they give drink to every beast of the field;
   the wild asses quench their thirst.
By them the birds of the air have their habitation;
   they sing among the branches.
From thy lofty abode thou waterest the mountains;
   the earth is satisfied with the fruit of thy work.

Thou dost cause the grass to grow for the cattle,
   and plants for man to cultivate,
that he may bring forth food from the earth.
Thou hast made the moon to mark the seasons;
   the sun knows its time for setting.
Thou makest darkness, and it is night,
   when all the beasts of the forest creep forth.
The young lions roar for their prey,
   seeking their food from God.
When the sun rises, they get them away
   and lie down in their dens.

122

Man goes forth to his work
  and to his labor until the evening.

O Lord, how manifold are thy works!
  In wisdom hast thou made them all;
  the earth is full of thy creatures.
Yonder is the sea, great and wide,
  which teems with things innumerable,
  living things both small and great.
These all look to thee,
  to give them their food in due season.
Bless the Lord, O my soul!
Praise the Lord!

From Psalms 104: 1–4, 10–14, 19–25, 27, 35.

I lift up my eyes to the hills.
  From whence does my help come?
My help comes from the Lord,
  who made heaven and earth.

He will not let your foot be moved,
  he who keeps you will not slumber.
Behold, he who keeps Israel
  will neither slumber nor sleep.

The Lord is your keeper;
  the Lord is your shade
  on your right hand.
The sun shall not smite you by day,
  nor the moon by night.

The LORD will keep you from all evil;
   he will keep your life.
The LORD will keep
   your going out and your coming in
   from this time forth and for evermore.

Psalms 121: 1–8.

O LORD, thou hast searched me and known me!
Thou knowest when I sit down and when I rise
     up;
   thou discernest my thoughts from afar.
Thou searchest out my path and my lying down,
   and art acquainted with all my ways.
Even before a word is on my tongue,
   lo, O LORD, thou knowest it altogether.
Search me, O God, and know my heart!
   Try me and know my thoughts!
And see if there be any wicked way in me,
   and lead me in the way everlasting!

From Psalms 139: 1–4, 23, 24.

Proverbs

Trust in the LORD with all your heart,
    and do not rely on your own insight.
In all your ways acknowledge him,
    and he will make straight your paths.

Proverbs 3: 5–6.

Go to the ant, O sluggard;
    consider her ways, and be wise.
Without having any chief,
    officer or ruler,
she prepares her food in summer,
    and gathers her sustenance in harvest.

Proverbs 6: 6–8.

I passed by the field of a sluggard,
    by the vineyard of a man without sense;
and lo, it was all overgrown with thorns;
    the ground was covered with nettles,
    and its stone wall was broken down.
Then I saw and considered it;
    I looked and received instruction.

125

"A little sleep, a little slumber,
  a little folding of the hands to rest,"
and poverty will come upon you like a robber,
  and want like an armed man.

Proverbs 24: 30–34.

A wise son makes a glad father,
  but a foolish son is a sorrow to his mother.

Proverbs 10: 1.

The way of a fool is right in his own eyes,
  but a wise man listens to advice.
The vexation of a fool is known at once,
  but the prudent man ignores an insult.

Proverbs 12: 15–16.

He who walks with wise men becomes wise,
  but the companion of fools will suffer harm.

Proverbs 13: 20.

Righteousness exalts a nation,
  but sin is a reproach to any people.
Proverbs 14: 34.

A soft answer turns away wrath,
  but a harsh word stirs up anger.
Proverbs 15: 1.

Pride goes before destruction,
  and a haughty spirit before a fall.
Proverbs 16: 18.

He who is slow to anger is better than the mighty,
and he who rules his spirit than he who takes a city.
Proverbs 16: 32

Better is a dry morsel with quiet
  than a house full of feasting with strife.
Proverbs 17: 1.

A friend loves at all times,
and a brother is born for adversity.

Proverbs 17: 17.

Even a child makes himself known by his acts,
whether what he does is pure and right.
The hearing ear and the seeing eye,
the LORD has made them both.

Proverbs 20: 11–12.

Wine is a mocker, strong drink a brawler;
and whoever is led astray by it is not wise.

Proverbs 20: 1.

Every way of a man is right in his own eyes,
but the LORD weighs the heart.

Proverbs 21: 2.

A good name is to be chosen rather than great riches.

From Proverbs 22: 1.

Do not look at wine when it is red,
when it sparkles in the cup
and goes down smoothly.
At the last it bites like a serpent,
and stings like an adder.
Your eyes will see strange things,
and your mind utter perverse things.

Proverbs 23: 31–33.

If your enemy is hungry, give him bread to eat;
and if he is thirsty, give him water to drink;
for you will heap coals of fire on his head,
and the LORD will reward you.

Proverbs 25: 21–22.

The Prophets Isaiah and Micah

In the year that King Uzzi'ah died I saw the Lord sitting upon a throne, high and lifted up. Above him stood the seraphim. And one called to another and said:

"Holy, holy, holy is the LORD of hosts;
the whole earth is full of his glory."

And the foundations of the thresholds shook at the voice of him who called, and the temple was filled with smoke. And I said: "Woe is me! For I am lost; for I am a man of unclean lips, and I dwell in the midst of a people of unclean lips; for my eyes have seen the King, the LORD of hosts!"

Then flew one of the seraphim to me, having in his hand a burning coal which he had taken with tongs from the altar. And he touched my mouth, and said: "Behold, this has touched your lips; your guilt is taken away, and your sin forgiven."

And I heard the voice of the Lord saying, "Whom shall I send, and who will go for us?"

Then I said, "Here I am! Send me."

From Isaiah 6: 1–8.

129

The Call to Repentance

The LORD has spoken:
"What to me is the multitude of your sacrifices?
I have had enough of burnt offerings of rams
    and the fat of fed beasts.
Bring no more vain offerings;
    incense is an abomination to me.
New moon and sabbath and the calling of assemblies—
    I cannot endure iniquity and solemn assembly.
Wash yourselves; make yourselves clean;
    remove the evil of your doings
    from before my eyes;
cease to do evil,
    learn to do good;
seek justice,
    correct oppression;
defend the fatherless,
    plead for the widow.
Come now, let us reason together,"
    says the LORD.
"Though your sins are like scarlet,
    they shall be as white as snow;
though they are red like crimson,
    they shall become like wool."

From Isaiah 1: 2, 11, 13, 16–18.

Woe to those
who trust in chariots because they are many
    and in horsemen because they are very strong,
but do not look to the Holy One of Israel
    or consult the LORD!

For thus said the Lord GOD, the Holy One of Israel,
"In returning and rest you shall be saved;
in quietness and in trust shall be your strength."
You will say in that day:
"Behold, God is my salvation;
I will trust, and will not be afraid;
for the LORD GOD is my strength and my song,
and he has become my salvation."

From Isaiah 31: 1; 30: 15; 12: 1–2.

The Prince of Peace

In the latter time the Lord will make glorious the way
of the sea, the land beyond the Jordan, Galilee of the
nations.

The people who walked in darkness
have seen a great light;
those who dwelt in a land of deep darkness,
on them has light shined.
Thou hast multiplied the nation,
thou hast increased its joy;
they rejoice before thee
as with joy at the harvest.

131

For to us a child is born,
    to us a son is given;
and the government will be upon his shoulder,
    and his name will be called
"Wonderful Counselor, Mighty God,
    Everlasting Father, Prince of Peace."
Of the increase of his government and of peace
    there will be no end,
upon the throne of David, and over his kingdom,
    to establish it, and to uphold it
with justice and with righteousness
    from this time forth and for evermore.

From Isaiah 9: 1–3, 6–7.

The Spirit of the Lord shall rest upon him,
    the spirit of wisdom and understanding,
    the spirit of counsel and might,
    the spirit of knowledge and the fear of the Lord.
And his delight shall be in the fear of the Lord.

132

He shall not judge by what his eyes see,
  or decide by what his ears hear;
but with righteousness he shall judge the poor,
  and decide with equity for the meek of the earth.
The wolf shall dwell with the lamb,
  and the leopard shall lie down with the kid,
and the calf and the lion and the fatling together,
  and a little child shall lead them.
The cow and the bear shall feed;
  their young shall lie down together.
They shall not hurt or destroy
  in all my holy mountain;
for the earth shall be full of the knowledge of the Lord
  as the waters cover the sea.

From Isaiah 11: 1–4, 6–7, 9.

Thou dost keep him in perfect peace,
  whose mind is stayed on thee,
  because he trusts in thee.

Isaiah 26: 3.

Peace After Suffering
Comfort, comfort my people,
  says your God.
Speak tenderly to Jerusalem,
  and cry to her
that her warfare is ended,
  that her iniquity is pardoned,
that she has received from the Lord's hand
  double for all her sins.

133

A voice cries:
"In the wilderness prepare the way of the LORD,
   make straight in the desert a highway for our God.
Every valley shall be lifted up,
   and every mountain and hill be made low;
the uneven ground shall become level,
   and the rough places a plain.
And the glory of the LORD shall be revealed,
   and all flesh shall see it together,
   for the mouth of the LORD has spoken."
Lift up your voice with strength,
   O Jerusalem, herald of good tidings,
   lift it up, fear not;
say to the cities of Judah,
   "Behold your God!"
He will feed his flock like a shepherd,
   he will gather the lambs in his arms,
he will carry them in his bosom,
   and gently lead those that are with young.

From Isaiah 40: 1–5, 9, 11.

The Greatness of God

Who has measured the waters in the hollow of his hand
and marked off the heavens with a span,
enclosed the dust of the earth in a measure
and weighed the mountains in scales
and the hills in a balance?
Have you not known? Have you not heard?
Has it not been told you from the beginning?
Have you not understood from the foundations of
the earth?
The LORD is the everlasting God,
the Creator of the ends of the earth.
He does not faint or grow weary,
his understanding is unsearchable.
He gives power to the faint,
and to him who has no might he increases strength.
Even youths shall faint and be weary,
and young men shall fall exhausted;
but they who wait for the LORD shall renew their
strength,
they shall mount up with wings like eagles,
they shall run and not be weary,
they shall walk and not faint.

From Isaiah 40: 12, 21, 28–31.

The Suffering Servant of God

Behold my servant, whom I uphold,
my chosen, in whom my soul delights;
I have put my spirit upon him,
he will bring forth justice to the nations.

135

He will not cry or lift up his voice,
  or make it heard in the street.
He will not fail or be discouraged
  till he has established justice in the earth.
Surely he has borne our griefs
  and carried our sorrows;
yet we esteemed him stricken,
  smitten by God, and afflicted.
But he was wounded for our transgressions,
  he was bruised for our iniquities;
upon him was the chastisement that made us whole,
  and with his stripes we are healed.
All we like sheep have gone astray;
  we have turned every one to his own way;
and the LORD has laid on him
  the iniquity of us all.

From Isaiah 42: 1–2, 4; 53: 4–6.

God's Call to His People
"Seek the LORD while he may be found,
  call upon him while he is near;
let the wicked forsake his way,
  and the unrighteous man his thoughts;
let him return to the LORD, that he may have mercy
    on him,
  and to our God, for he will abundantly pardon.
For my thoughts are not your thoughts,
  neither are your ways my ways, says the LORD.
For as the heavens are higher than the earth,
  so are my ways higher than your ways
  and my thoughts than your thoughts.

"For as the rain and the snow come down from heaven,
   and return not thither but water the earth,
making it bring forth and sprout,
   giving seed to the sower and bread to the eater,
so shall my word be that goes forth from my mouth;
   it shall not return to me empty,
but it shall accomplish that which I purpose,
   and prosper in the thing for which I sent it.

"For you shall go out in joy,
   and be led forth in peace;
the mountains and the hills before you
   shall break forth into singing,
   and all the trees of the field shall clap their hands.
Instead of the thorn shall come up the cypress;
   instead of the brier shall come up the myrtle;
and it shall be to the LORD for a memorial,
   for an everlasting sign which shall not be cut off."

From Isaiah 55: 6–13.

he Word of the LORD to Micah

The word of the LORD that came to Micah, which he
saw concerning Samar'ia and Jerusalem.
   It shall come to pass in the latter days
      that the mountain of the house of the LORD
   shall be established as the highest of the mountains,
      and shall be raised up above the hills;
   and peoples shall flow to it,
      and many nations shall come, and say:
"Come, let us go up to the mountain of the LORD,
      to the house of the God of Jacob;
   that he may teach us his ways
      and we may walk in his paths."

For out of Zion shall go forth the law,
  and the word of the LORD from Jerusalem.
He shall judge between many peoples,
  and shall decide for strong nations afar off;
and they shall beat their swords into plowshares,
  and their spears into pruning hooks;
nation shall not lift up sword against nation,
  neither shall they learn war any more;
but they shall sit every man under his vine and under
    his fig tree,
  and none shall make them afraid;
  for the mouth of the LORD of hosts has spoken.

"With what shall I come before the LORD,
  and bow myself before God on high?
He has showed you, O man, what is good;
  and what does the LORD require of you
but to do justice, and to love kindness,
  and to walk humbly with your God?"

From Micah 1: 1; 4: 1–4; 6: 6, 8.

New Testament

The Early Life of Jesus

In the days of Herod, king of Judea, there was a priest named Zechari'ah; and he had a wife whose name was Elizabeth. And they were both righteous before God, walking in all the commandments and ordinances of the Lord blameless. But they had no child, because Elizabeth was barren, and both were advanced in years.

Now while Zechari'ah was serving as priest before God when his division was on duty, according to the custom of the priesthood, it fell to him by lot to enter the temple of the Lord and burn incense. And the whole multitude of the people were praying outside. And there appeared to him an angel of the Lord standing on the right side of the altar of incense. Zechari'ah was troubled when he saw him, and fear fell upon him. But the angel said to him, "Do not be afraid, Zechari'ah, for your prayer is heard, and your wife Elizabeth will bear you a son, and you shall call his name John.

And you will have joy and gladness,
  and many will rejoice at his birth;
  for he will be great before the Lord,

141

and he shall drink no wine nor strong drink,
and he will be filled with the Holy Spirit,
even from his mother's womb.
He will turn many of the sons of Israel to the Lord
their God,
and he will go before him in the spirit and power of
Eli'jah,
to turn the hearts of the fathers to the children,
and the disobedient to the wisdom of the just,
to make ready for the Lord a people prepared."

Now the time came for Elizabeth to be delivered, and she gave birth to a son. And her neighbors and kinsfolk heard that the Lord had shown great mercy to her, and they rejoiced with her. On the eighth day they came to circumcise the child; and they would have named him Zechari'ah after his father, but his mother said, "Not so; he shall be called John."

And the child grew and became strong in spirit, and he was in the wilderness till the day of his manifestation to Israel.

From Luke 1: 5–17, 57–60, 80.

Jesus Is Born

The angel Gabriel was sent from God to a city of Galilee named Nazareth, to a virgin betrothed to a man whose name was Joseph, of the house of David; and the virgin's name was Mary. And he came to her and said, "Hail, O favored One, the Lord is with you!" But she was greatly troubled at the saying, and considered in her mind what sort of greeting this might be.

And the angel said to her, "Do not be afraid, Mary, for you have found favor with God. And behold, you will conceive in your womb and bear a son, and you shall call his name Jesus.

> "He will be great, and will be called the Son of the
> Most High;
> and the Lord God will give to him the throne of his
> father David,
> and he will reign over the house of Jacob for ever;
> and of his kingdom there will be no end."

And Mary said to the angel, "How can this be, since I have no husband?"

And the angel said to her,

> "The Holy Spirit will come upon you,
> and the power of the Most High will overshadow you;
> therefore the child to be born will be called holy,
> the Son of God."

And Mary said, "Behold I am the handmaid of the Lord; let it be to me according to your word." And the angel departed from her.

In those days a decree went out from Caesar Augustus that all the world should be enrolled. This was the first enrollment, when Quirin'i-us was governor of Syria. And all went to be enrolled, each to his own city. And Joseph went up from Galilee, from the city of Nazareth, to Judea, to the city of David, which is called Bethlehem, because he was of the house and lineage of David, to be enrolled with Mary, his betrothed, who was with child. And while they were there, the time came for her to be delivered. And she gave birth to her first-born son and wrapped him in swaddling cloths, and laid him in a manger, because there was no place for them in the inn.

From Luke 1: 26–35, 38; 2: 1–7.

Those Who Heard the Good News

And in that region there were shepherds out in the field, keeping watch over their flock by night. And an angel of the Lord appeared to them, and the glory of the Lord shone around them, and they were filled with fear.

And the angel said to them, "Be not afraid; for behold, I bring you good news of a great joy which will come to all the people; for to you is born this day in the city of David a Savior, who is Christ the Lord. And this will be a sign for you: you will find a babe wrapped in swaddling cloths and lying in a manger."

And suddenly there was with the angel a multitude of the heavenly host praising God and saying,

"Glory to God in the highest,
  and on earth peace among men with whom he is
    pleased!"

When the angels went away from them into heaven, the shepherds said to one another, "Let us go over to Bethlehem and see this thing that has happened, which the Lord has made known to us."

And they went with haste, and found Mary and Joseph, and the babe lying in a manger. And when they saw it they made known the saying which had been told them concerning this child; and all who heard it wondered at what the shepherds told them. But Mary kept all these things, pondering them in her heart. And the shepherds returned, glorifying and praising God for all they had heard and seen, as it had been told them.

And at the end of eight days, when he was circumcised, the babe was called Jesus, the name given by the angel before he was conceived in the womb.

And when the time came for their purification accord-

ing to the law of Moses, they brought him up to Jerusalem to present him to the Lord, and to offer a sacrifice according to what is said in the law of the Lord, "a pair of turtledoves, or two young pigeons."

Now there was a man in Jerusalem, whose name was Simeon, and this man was righteous and devout, looking for the consolation of Israel. And inspired by the Spirit he came into the temple; and when the parents brought in the child Jesus, to do for him according to the custom of the law, he took him up in his arms and blessed God and said,

"Lord, now lettest thou thy servant depart in peace,
according to thy word;
for mine eyes have seen thy salvation
which thou has prepared in the presence of all
peoples,
a light for revelation to the Gentiles,
and for glory to thy people Israel."

And his father and his mother marveled at what was said about him.

Now when Jesus was born in Bethlehem of Judea in the days of Herod the king, behold, wise men from the East came to Jerusalem, saying, "Where is he who has

been born king of the Jews? For we have seen his star in the East, and have come to worship him."

When Herod the king heard this, he was troubled, and all Jerusalem with him; and assembling all the chief priests and scribes of the people, he inquired of them where the Christ was to be born. They told him, "In Bethlehem of Judea; for so it is written by the prophet:

'And you, O Bethlehem, in the land of Judah,
  are by no means least among the rulers of Judah;
  for from you shall come a ruler
  who will govern my people Israel.' "

Then Herod summoned the wise men secretly and ascertained from them what time the star appeared; and he sent them to Bethlehem, saying, "Go and search diligently for the child, and when you have found him bring me word, that I too may come and worship him."

When they had heard the king they went their way; and lo, the star which they had seen in the East went before them, till it came to rest over the place where the child was. When they saw the star, they rejoiced exceedingly with great joy; and going into the house they saw the child with Mary his mother, and they fell down and worshiped him. Then, opening their treasures, they offered him gifts, gold and frankincense and myrrh. And being warned in a dream not to return to Herod, they departed to their own country by another way.

From Luke 2: 8–22, 24–25, 27–33; Matthew 2: 1–12.

The Boyhood of Jesus

Now when the wise men had departed, behold, an angel of the Lord appeared to Joseph in a dream and said, "Rise, take the child and his mother, and flee to Egypt, and remain there till I tell you; for Herod is about to search for the child, to destroy him." And he took the child and his mother by night, and departed to Egypt.

Then Herod, when he saw that he had been tricked by the wise men, was in a furious rage, and he sent and killed all the male children in Bethlehem and in all that region who were two years old or under, according to the time which he had ascertained from the wise men.

But when Herod died, behold, an angel of the Lord appeared in a dream to Joseph in Egypt, saying, "Rise, take the child and his mother, and go to the land of Israel, for those who sought the child's life are dead." And he rose and took the child and his mother, and went to the land of Israel. But when he heard that Archela'us reigned over Judea in place of his father Herod, he was afraid to go there, and being warned in a dream he withdrew to the district of Galilee. And he went and dwelt in a city called Nazareth.

And the child grew and became strong, filled with wisdom; and the favor of God was upon him.

Now his parents went to Jerusalem every year at the feast of the Passover. And when he was twelve years old, they went up according to custom; and when the feast

was ended, as they were returning, the boy Jesus stayed behind in Jerusalem. His parents did not know it, but supposing him to be in the company they went a day's journey, and they sought him among their kinsfolk and acquaintances; and when they did not find him, they returned to Jerusalem, seeking him.

After three days they found him in the temple, sitting among the teachers, listening to them and asking them questions; and all who heard him were amazed at his understanding and his answers. And when they saw him

they were astonished; and his mother said to him, "Son, why have you treated us so? Behold, your father and I have been looking for you anxiously."

And he said to them, "How is it that you sought me? Did you not know that I must be in my Father's house?"

And they did not understand the saying which he spoke to them. And he went down with them and came to Nazareth, and was obedient to them; and his mother kept all these things in her heart.

And Jesus increased in wisdom and in stature, and in favor with God and man.

From Matthew 2: 13–14, 16, 19–23; Luke 2: 40–52.

John Baptizes Jesus

In those days came John the Baptist, preaching in the wilderness of Judea, "Repent, for the kingdom of heaven is at hand." For this is he who was spoken of by the prophet Isaiah when he said,

"The voice of one crying in the wilderness:
Prepare the way of the Lord,
make his paths straight."

Now John wore a garment of camel's hair, and a leather girdle around his waist; and his food was locusts and wild honey. Then went out to him Jerusalem and all Judea and all the region about the Jordan, and they were baptized by him in the river Jordan, confessing their sins.

And the multitudes asked, "What then shall we do?"

And he answered them, "He who has two coats, let him share with him who has none; and he who has food, let him do likewise."

Tax collectors also came to be baptized, and said to him, "Teacher, what shall we do?"

151

And he said to them, "Collect no more than is appointed you."

Soldiers also asked him, "And we, what shall we do?"

And he said to them, "Rob no one by violence or by false accusation, and be content with your wages."

So, with many other exhortations, he preached good news to the people, saying, "After me comes he who is mightier than I, the thong of whose sandals I am not worthy to stoop down and untie. I have baptized you with water; but he will baptize you with the Holy Spirit."

Jesus, when he began his ministry, was about thirty years of age. Then he came from Galilee to the Jordan to John, to be baptized by him. John would have prevented him, saying, "I need to be baptized by you, and do you come to me?"

But Jesus answered him, "Let it be so now; for thus it is fitting for us to fulfil all righteousness."

And Jesus was baptized by John in the Jordan. When he came up out of the water, immediately he saw the heavens opened and the Spirit descending upon him like a dove; and a voice came from heaven, "Thou art my beloved Son; with thee I am well pleased."

The Spirit immediately drove him out into the wilderness. And he was in the wilderness forty days, tempted by Satan; and he was with the wild beasts; and the angels ministered to him.

But Herod the tetrarch, who had been reproved by John for Hero'di-as, his brother's wife, and for all the evil things that Herod had done, added this to them all, that he shut up John in prison.

From Matthew 3: 1–6; Luke 3: 10–14, 18; Mark 1: 7–8; Luke 3: 23; Matthew 3: 13–15; Mark 1: 9–13; Luke 3: 19–20.

The People Heard Him Gladly

Now after John was arrested, Jesus came into Galilee, preaching the gospel of God.

And he came to Nazareth, where he had been brought up; and he went to the synagogue, as his custom was, on the sabbath day. And he stood up to read; and there was given to him the book of the prophet Isaiah. He opened the book and found the place where it was written,

"The Spirit of the Lord is upon me,
    because he has anointed me to preach good news to
      the poor.
    He has sent me to proclaim release to the captives
    and recovering of sight to the blind,
    to set at liberty those who are oppressed,
    to proclaim the acceptable year of the Lord."

And he closed the book, and gave it back to the attendant, and sat down; and the eyes of all in the synagogue were fixed on him.

And he began to say to them, "Today this scripture has been fulfilled in your hearing."

And all spoke well of him, and wondered at the gracious words which proceeded out of his mouth; and they said, "Is not this Joseph's son?"

From Mark 1: 14; Luke 4: 16–22.

By the Sea of Galilee

And passing along by the Sea of Galilee, Jesus saw Simon and Andrew the brother of Simon casting a net in the sea; for they were fishermen.

And Jesus said to them, "Follow me and I will make you become fishers of men."

And immediately they left their nets and followed him. And going on a little farther, he saw James the son of Zeb'edee and John his brother, who were in their boat mending the nets. And immediately he called them; and they left their father Zeb'edee in the boat with the hired servants, and followed him.

And they went into Caper'na-um; and immediately on the sabbath Jesus entered the synagogue and taught. And they were astonished at his teaching, for he taught them as one who had authority, and not as the scribes. And at once his fame spread everywhere throughout all the surrounding region of Galilee.

And he left the synagogue, and entered the house of Simon and Andrew, with James and John. Now Simon's mother-in-law lay sick with a fever, and immediately they told him of her. And he took her by the hand and lifted her up, and the fever left her; and she served them.

That evening, at sundown, they brought to him all who were sick or possessed with demons. The whole city was gathered about the door. And he healed many who were sick, and cast out many demons.

And in the morning, a great while before day, he rose

and went out to a lonely place, and there he prayed. Simon and those who were with Jesus followed him, and said, "Every one is searching for you."

And he said to them, "Let us go on to the next towns, that I may preach there also; for that is why I came out."

And Jesus went about all Galilee, teaching in their synagogues and preaching the gospel of the kingdom and healing every disease and every infirmity among the people. Great crowds followed him from Galiliee and the Decap'olis and Jerusalem and Judea and beyond the Jordan.

From Mark 1: 16–22, 28–38; Matthew 4: 23, 25.

The Beatitudes

Seeing the crowds, Jesus went up on the mountain, and when he sat down his disciples came to him. And he opened his mouth and taught them, saying:

"Blessed are the poor in spirit, for theirs is the kingdom of heaven.

"Blessed are those who mourn, for they shall be comforted.

"Blessed are the meek, for they shall inherit the earth.

"Blessed are those who hunger and thirst for righteousness, for they shall be satisfied.

"Blessed are the merciful, for they shall obtain mercy.

"Blessed are the pure in heart, for they shall see God.

"Blessed are the peacemakers, for they shall be called sons of God.

"Blessed are those who are persecuted for righteousness' sake, for theirs is the kingdom of heaven.

"Blessed are you when men revile you and persecute you and utter all kinds of evil against you falsely on my

account. Rejoice and be glad, for your reward is great in heaven, for so men persecuted the prophets who were before you."

From Matthew 5: 1–12.

Jesus Teaches the People

"You are the salt of the earth; but if salt has lost its taste, how shall its saltness be restored? It is no longer good for anything except to be thrown out and trodden under foot by men.

"You are the light of the world. A city set on a hill cannot be hid. Nor do men light a lamp and put it under a bushel, but on a stand, and it gives light to all in the house. Let your light so shine before men, that they may see your good works and give glory to your Father who is in heaven.

"Again you have heard that it was said to the men of old, 'You shall not swear falsely, but shall perform to the Lord what you have sworn.' But I say to you, Do not swear at all, either by heaven, for it is the throne of God, or by the earth, for it is his footstool, or by Jerusalem, for it is the city of the great King. And do not swear by your head, for you cannot make one hair white or black. Let what you say be simply 'Yes' or 'No'; anything more than this comes from evil.

"You have heard that it was said, 'An eye for an eye and a tooth for a tooth.' But I say to you, Do not resist one who is evil. But if any one strikes you on the right cheek, turn to him the other also; and if any one would sue you and take your coat, let him have your cloak as well; and if any one forces you to go one mile, go with him two miles. Give to him who begs from you, and do not refuse him who would borrow from you.

158

"You have heard that it was said, 'You shall love your neighbor and hate your enemy.' But I say to you, Love your enemies and pray for those who persecute you, so that you may be sons of your Father who is in heaven; for he makes his sun rise on the evil and on the good, and sends rain on the just and on the unjust. For if you love those who love you, what reward have you? Do not even the tax collectors do the same? And if you salute only your brethren, what more are you doing than others? Do

not even the Gentiles do the same? You, therefore, must be perfect, as your heavenly Father is perfect.

"Therefore I tell you, do not be anxious about your life, what you shall eat or what you shall drink, nor about your body, what you shall put on. Is not life more than food, and the body more than clothing?

"Look at the birds of the air: they neither sow nor reap nor gather into barns, and yet your heavenly Father feeds them. Are you not of more value than they?

"And which of you by being anxious can add one cubit to his span of life? And why are you anxious about clothing? Consider the lilies of the field, how they grow; they neither toil nor spin; yet I tell you, even Solomon in all his glory was not arrayed like one of these. But if God so clothes the grass of the field, which today is alive and tomorrow is thrown into the oven, will he not much more clothe you, O men of little faith?

"Therefore do not be anxious, saying, 'What shall we eat?' or 'What shall we drink?' or 'What shall we wear?' For the Gentiles seek all these things; and your heavenly Father knows that you need them all. But seek first his kingdom and his righteousness, and all these things shall be yours as well.

"Therefore do not be anxious about tomorrow, for to-morrow will be anxious for itself. Let the day's own trouble be sufficient for the day.

"Judge not, that you be not judged. For with the judg-

ment you pronounce you will be judged, and the measure you give will be the measure you get. Why do you see the speck that is in your brother's eye, but do not notice the log that is in your own eye? Or how can you say to your brother, 'Let me take the speck out of your eye,' when there is the log in your own eye?

"So whatever you wish that men would do to you, do so to them; for this is the law and the prophets.

"No good tree bears bad fruit, nor again does a bad tree bear good fruit; for each tree is known by its own fruit. For figs are not gathered from thorns, nor are grapes picked from a bramble bush. The good man out of the good treasure of his heart produces good, and the evil man out of his evil treasure produces evil; for out of the abundance of the heart his mouth speaks.

"Every one then who hears these words of mine and does them will be like a wise man who built his house upon the rock; and the rain fell, and the floods came, and the winds blew and beat upon that house, but it did not fall, because it had been founded on the rock. And every one who hears these words of mine and does not do them will be like a foolish man who built his house upon the sand; and the rain fell, and the floods came, and the winds blew and beat against that house, and it fell; and great was the fall of it."

And when Jesus finished these sayings, the crowds were astonished at his teaching, for he taught them as one who had authority, and not as their scribes.

From Matthew 5: 13–16, 33–48; 6: 25–34; 7: 1–4, 12; Luke 6: 43–45;
Matthew 7: 24–29.

The Lord's Prayer

Jesus was praying in a certain place, and when he ceased, one of his disciples said to him, "Lord, teach us to pray, as John taught his disciples." And he said to them, "When you pray, say:

Our Father who art in heaven,
Hallowed be thy name.
Thy kingdom come,
Thy will be done,
    On earth as it is in heaven.
Give us this day our daily bread;
And forgive us our debts,
    As we also have forgiven our debtors;
And lead us not into temptation,
    But deliver us from evil.

For thine is the kingdom and the power and the glory, for ever. Amen."

From Luke 11: 1–2; Matthew 6: 9–13.

When Jesus Saw Their Faith

Jesus entered Caper'na-um. Now a centurion had a slave who was dear to him, who was sick and at the point of death. When he heard of Jesus, he sent to him elders of the Jews, asking him to come and heal his slave. And when they came to Jesus, they besought him earnestly, saying, "He is worthy to have you do this for him, for he loves our nation, and he built us our synagogue."

And Jesus went with them. When he was not far from the house, the centurion sent friends to him, saying to him, "Lord, do not trouble yourself, for I am not worthy to have you come under my roof; therefore I did not presume to come to you. But say the word, and let my servant be healed. For I am a man under authority, with soldiers under me: and I say to one, 'Go,' and he goes; and to another, 'Come,' and he comes; and to my slave, 'Do this,' and he does it."

When Jesus heard this he marveled at him, and turned and said to the multitude that followed him, "I tell you, not even in Israel have I found such faith." And when those who had been sent returned to the house, they found the slave well.

One day, as Jesus was teaching, there were Pharisees

and teachers of the law sitting by, who had come from every village of Galilee and Judea and from Jerusalem; and the power of the Lord was with him to heal.

And behold, men were bringing on a bed a man who was paralyzed, and they sought to bring him in and lay him before Jesus; but finding no way to bring him in, because of the crowd, they went up on the roof and let him down with his bed through the tiles into the midst before Jesus.

And when he saw their faith he said, "Man, your sins are forgiven you."

And the scribes and the Pharisees began to question, saying, "Who is this that speaks blasphemies? Who can forgive sins but God only?"

When Jesus perceived their questionings, he answered them, "Why do you question in your hearts? Which is easier, to say, 'Your sins are forgiven you,' or to say, 'Rise and walk'? But that you may know that the Son of man has authority on earth to forgive sins"—he said to the man who was paralyzed—"I say to you, rise, take up your bed and go home."

And immediately he rose before them, and took up that on which he lay, and went home, glorifying God. And amazement seized them all, and they glorified God and were filled with awe, saying, "We have seen strange things today."

From Luke 7: 1–10; 5: 17–26.

Jesus Chooses Twelve Apostles

As Jesus passed on from there, he saw a man called Matthew sitting at the tax office; and he said to him, "Follow me." And Matthew rose and followed Jesus.

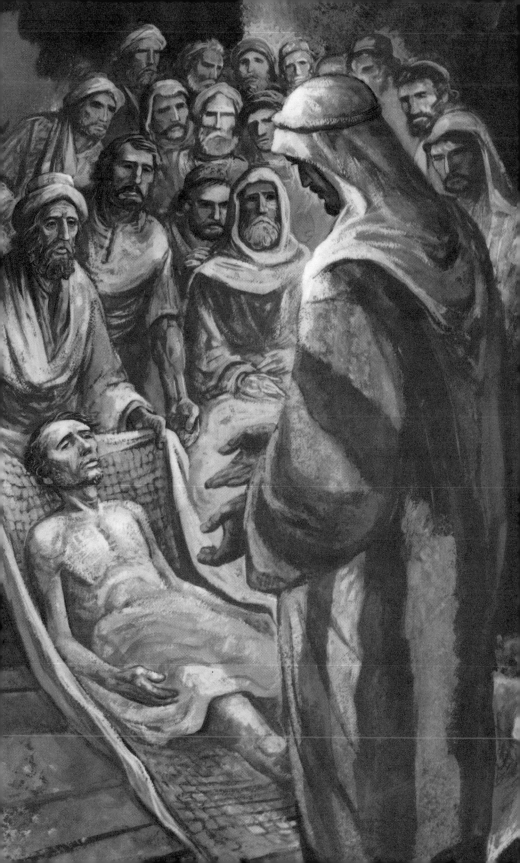

And as he sat at table in the house, behold, many tax collectors and sinners came and sat down with Jesus and his disciples. And when the Pharisees saw this, they said to his disciples, "Why does your teacher eat with tax collectors and sinners?"

But when Jesus heard it, he said, "Those who are well have no need of a physician, but those who are sick. Go and learn what this means, 'I desire mercy, and not sacrifice.' For I came not to call the righteous, but sinners."

In these days Jesus went out into the hills to pray; and all night he continued in prayer to God. And when it was day, he called his disciples, and chose from them twelve, whom he named apostles; Simon, whom he named Peter, and Andrew his brother, and James and John, and Philip, and Bartholomew, and Matthew, and Thomas, and James the son of Alphaeus, and Simon who was called the Zealot, and Judas the son of James, and Judas Iscariot, who became a traitor.

And he called the twelve together and gave them power and authority over all demons and to cure diseases, and he sent them out to preach the kingdom of God and to heal. And he said to them, "Take no gold, nor silver, nor copper in your belts, no bag for your journey, nor two tunics, nor sandals, nor a staff; for the laborer deserves his food. And whatever town or village you enter, find out who is worthy in it, and stay with him until you depart. As you enter the house, salute it."

And they departed and went through the villages, preaching the gospel and healing everywhere.

From Matthew 9: 9–13; Luke 6: 12–16; 9: 1–3; Matthew 10: 9–12; Luke 9: 6.

Jesus Meets Opposition

One sabbath Jesus was going through the grainfields; and as they made their way his disciples began to pluck ears of grain. And the Pharisees said to him, "Look, why are they doing what is not lawful on the sabbath?"

And Jesus said to them, "Have you never read what David did, when he was in need and was hungry, he and those who were with him: how he entered the house of God, when Abi'athar was high priest, and ate the bread of the Presence, which it is not lawful for any but the priests to eat, and also gave it to those who were with him?" And he said to them, "The sabbath was made for man, not man for the sabbath; so the Son of man is lord even of the sabbath."

Again Jesus entered the synagogue, and a man was there who had a withered hand. And they watched him, to see whether he would heal him on the sabbath, so that they might accuse him. And he said to the man who had the withered hand, "Come here."

And he said to them, "Is it lawful on the sabbath to do good or to do harm, to save life or to kill?"

167

But they were silent. And he looked around at them with anger, grieved at their hardness of heart, and said to the man, "Stretch out your hand." He stretched it out, and his hand was restored. The Pharisees went out, and immediately held counsel with the Hero'di-ans against Jesus, how to destroy him.

From Mark 2: 23–28; 3: 1–6.

The Parable of the Sower

Jesus went out and sat beside the sea. And great crowds gathered about him, so that he got into a boat and sat there; and the whole crowd stood on the beach.

And he told them many things in parables, saying: "A sower went out to sow. And as he sowed, some seeds fell along the path, and the birds came and devoured them. Other seeds fell on rocky ground, where they had not much soil, and immediately they sprang up, since they had no depth of soil, but when the sun rose they were scorched; and since they had no root they withered away. Other seeds fell upon thorns, and the thorns grew up and choked them. Other seeds fell on good soil and brought forth grain, some a hundredfold, some sixty, some thirty.

"Hear then the parable of the sower. When any one hears the word of the kingdom and does not understand it, the evil one comes and snatches away what is sown in his heart; this is what was sown along the path.

"As for what was sown on rocky ground, this is he who hears the word and immediately receives it with joy; yet he has no root in himself, but endures for a while, and when tribulation or persecution arises on account of the word, immediately he falls away.

"As for what was sown among thorns, this is he who

168

hears the word, but the cares of the world and the delight in riches choke the word, and it proves unfruitful.

"As for what was sown on good soil, this is he who hears the word and understands it; he indeed bears fruit, and yields, in one case a hundredfold, in another sixty, and in another thirty."

From Matthew 13: 1–8, 18–23.

Jesus Rejected at Nazareth

Jesus went away from there and came to his own country; and his disciples followed him. And on the sabbath he began to teach in the synagogue; and many who heard him were astonished, saying, "Where did this man get all this? What is the wisdom given to him? What mighty works are wrought by his hands! Is not this the carpenter, the son of Mary and brother of James and Joses and Judas and Simon, and are not his sisters here with us?"

And they took offense at him. And Jesus said to them, "A prophet is not without honor, except in his own country, and among his own kin, and in his own house."

And he could do no mighty work there, except that he laid his hands upon a few sick people and healed them. And he marveled because of their unbelief.

And he went about among the villages teaching.

From Mark 6: 1–6.

"Give Them Something to Eat"

Jesus said to the disciples, "Come away by yourselves to a lonely place, and rest a while." For many were coming and going, and they had no leisure even to eat. And they went away in the boat to a lonely place by themselves. Now many saw them going, and knew them, and

170

they ran there on foot from all the towns, and got there ahead of them.

As he landed he saw a great throng, and he had compassion on them, because they were like sheep without a shepherd; and he began to teach them many things.

And when it grew late, his disciples came to him and said, "This is a lonely place, and the hour is now late; send them away, to go into the country and villages round about and buy themselves something to eat." But Jesus answered them, "You give them something to eat."

And they said to him, "Shall we go and buy two hundred denarii worth of bread, and give it to them to eat?"

And he said to them, "How many loaves have you?"

And they said, "Five, and two fish."

Then Jesus commanded them all to sit down by companies upon the green grass. So they sat down in groups, by hundreds and by fifties. And taking the five loaves and the two fish he looked up to heaven, and blessed, and broke the loaves, and gave them to the disciples to set before the people; and he divided the two fish among them all. And they all ate and were satisfied. And they took up twelve baskets full of broken pieces and of the fish. And those who ate were five thousand men.

From Mark 6: 31–44.

"You Are the Christ"

Now when Jesus came into the district of Caesare'a Philippi, he asked his disciples, "Who do men say that the Son of man is?"

And they said, "Some say John the Baptist, others say Eli'jah, and others Jeremiah or one of the prophets."

He said to them, "But who do you say that I am?"

Simon Peter replied, "You are the Christ, the Son of the living God."

And Jesus answered him, "Blessed are you, Simon Bar-Jona! For flesh and blood has not revealed this to you, but my Father who is in heaven. You are Peter, and on this rock I will build my church, and the powers of death shall not prevail against it."

Then he strictly charged the disciples to tell no one that he was the Christ.

From that time Jesus began to show his disciples that he must go to Jerusalem and suffer many things from the elders and chief priests and scribes, and be killed, and on the third day be raised. And Peter took him and began to rebuke him, saying, "God forbid, Lord! This shall never happen to you."

But Jesus turned and said to Peter, "Get behind me, Satan! You are a hindrance to me; for you are not on the side of God, but of men."

Now Jesus took with him Peter and John and James, and went up on the mountain to pray. And as he was praying, the appearance of his countenance was altered, and his raiment became dazzling white. A bright cloud overshadowed them, and a voice from the cloud said, "This is my beloved Son, with whom I am well pleased; listen to him."

172

When the disciples heard this, they fell on their faces, and were filled with awe. But Jesus came and touched them, saying, "Rise, and have no fear." And when they lifted up their eyes, they saw no one but Jesus only.

Jesus and the disciples went on from there and passed through Galilee. And he would not have any one know it; for he was teaching his disciples, saying to them, "The Son of man will be delivered into the hands of men, and they will kill him; and when he is killed, after three days he will rise." But they did not understand the saying, and they were afraid to ask him.

And Jesus said to all, "If any man would come after me, let him deny himself and take up his cross daily and follow me. For whoever would save his life will lose it; and whoever loses his life for my sake, he will save it. For what does it profit a man if he gains the whole world and loses or forfeits himself?

"Come to me, all who labor and are heavy-laden, and I will give you rest.

"Take my yoke upon you, and learn from me; for I am gentle and lowly in heart, and you will find rest for your souls. For my yoke is easy, and my burden is light."

From Matthew 16: 13–18, 20–23; Luke 9: 28–29; Matthew 17: 5–8; Mark 9: 30–32; Luke 9: 23–25; Matthew 11: 28–30.

Who Is the Greatest?

Jesus and the disciples came to Caper'na-um; and when he was in the house he asked them, "What were you discussing on the way?"

But they were silent; for on the way they had discussed with one another who was the greatest.

And he sat down and called the twelve; and he said to

them, "If any one would be first, he must be last of all and servant of all."

And he took a child, and put him in the midst of them; and taking him in his arms, he said to them, "Truly, I say to you, unless you turn and become like children, you will never enter the kingdom of heaven. Whoever humbles himself like this child, he is the greatest in the kingdom of heaven. Whoever receives one such child in my name receives me."

From Mark 9: 33–36; Matthew 18: 3–5.

What Is Forgiveness?

Jesus said, "If your brother sins against you, go and tell him his fault, between you and him alone. If he listens to you, you have gained your brother."

Then Peter came up and said to him, "Lord, how often shall my brother sin against me, and I forgive him? As many as seven times?"

Jesus said to him, "I do not say to you seven times, but seventy times seven. For if you forgive men their trespasses, your heavenly Father also will forgive you; but if you do not forgive men their trespasses, neither will your Father forgive your trespasses."

And Jesus told this parable, saying:

"A king wished to settle accounts with his servants. When he began the reckoning, one was brought to him who owed him ten thousand talents; and as he could not pay, his lord ordered him to be sold, with his wife and children and all that he had, and payment to be made.

"So the servant fell on his knees, imploring him, 'Lord, have patience with me, and I will pay you everything.' And out of pity for him the lord of that servant released him and forgave him the debt.

"But that same servant, as he went out, came upon one of his fellow servants who owed him a hundred denarii; and seizing him by the throat he said, 'Pay what you owe.' So his fellow servant fell down and besought him, 'Have patience with me, and I will pay you.' He refused and went and put him in prison till he should pay the debt.

"When his fellow servants saw what had taken place, they were greatly distressed, and they went and reported to their lord all that had taken place. Then his lord summoned him and said to him, 'You wicked servant! I forgave you all that debt because you besought me; and should not you have had mercy on your fellow servant, as I had mercy on you?' And in anger his lord delivered him to the jailers, till he should pay all his debt. So also my heavenly Father will do to every one of you, if you do not forgive your brother from your heart."

From Matthew 18: 15, 21–22; 6: 14–15; 18: 23–35.

The Good Samaritan

A lawyer stood up to put Jesus to the test, saying, "Teacher, what shall I do to inherit eternal life?"

He said to him, "What is written in the law?"

And he answered, "You shall love the Lord your God with all your heart, and with all your soul, and with all your strength, and with all your mind; and your neighbor as yourself."

And Jesus said to him, "You have answered right; do this, and you will live."

But the lawyer, desiring to justify himself, said to Jesus, "And who is my neighbor?"

Jesus replied, "A man was going down from Jerusalem to Jericho, and he fell among robbers, who stripped him and beat him, and departed, leaving him half-dead. Now by chance a priest was going down that road; and when he saw him he passed by on the other side. So likewise a Levite, when he came to the place and saw him, passed by on the other side. But a Samaritan, as he journeyed, came to where he was; and when he saw him, he had compassion, and went to him and bound up his wounds, pouring on oil and wine; then he set him on his own beast and brought him to an inn, and took care of him. And the next day he took out two denarii and gave them to the innkeeper, saying, 'Take care of him; and whatever more you spend, I will repay you when I come back.' Which of these three, do you think, proved neighbor to the man who fell among the robbers?"

He said, "The one who showed mercy on him."

And Jesus said to him, "Go and do likewise."

From Luke 10: 25–37.

The Rich Fool

One of the multitude said to him, "Teacher, bid my brother divide the inheritance with me."

But he said to him, "Man, who made me a judge or divider over you?"

And Jesus said to them, "Take heed, and beware of all covetousness; for a man's life does not consist in the abundance of his possessions."

And he told them a parable, saying, "The land of a rich man brought forth plentifully; and he thought to himself, 'What shall I do, for I have nowhere to store my crops?' And he said, 'I will do this: I will pull down my barns, and build larger ones; and there I will store all my grain and my goods. And I will say to my soul, Soul, you have ample goods laid up for many years; take your ease, eat, drink, be merry.' But God said to him, 'Fool! This night your soul is required of you; and the things you have prepared, whose will they be?' So is he who lays up treasure for himself, and is not rich toward God."

From Luke 12: 13–21.

The Lost Sheep and the Lost Coin

Now the tax collectors and sinners were all drawing near to hear Jesus. And the Pharisees and the scribes murmured, "This man receives sinners and eats with them."

So he told them this parable: "What man of you, having a hundred sheep, if he has lost one of them, does not leave the ninety-nine in the wilderness, and go after the one which is lost, until he finds it? And when he has found it, he lays it on his shoulders, rejoicing. And when

he comes home, he calls together his friends and his neighbors, saying to them, 'Rejoice with me, for I have found my sheep which was lost.' Even so, I tell you, there will be more joy in heaven over one sinner who repents than over ninety-nine righteous persons who need no repentance.

"Or what woman, having ten silver coins, if she loses one coin, does not light a lamp and sweep the house and seek diligently until she finds it? And when she has found it, she calls together her friends and neighbors, saying, 'Rejoice with me, for I have found the coin which I had lost.' Even so, I tell you, there is joy before the angels of God over one sinner who repents."

From Luke 15: 1–10.

The Forgiving Father

And Jesus said, "There was a man who had two sons; and the younger of them said to his father, 'Father, give me the share of property that falls to me.' And the father divided his living between them.

"Not many days later, the younger son gathered all he had and took his journey into a far country, and there he squandered his property in loose living. And when he had spent everything, a great famine arose in that country, and he began to be in want. So he went and joined himself to one of the citizens of that country, who sent him to feed swine. And he would gladly have fed on the pods that the swine ate; and no one gave him anything.

"But when he came to himself he said, 'How many of my father's hired servants have bread enough and to spare, but I perish here with hunger! I will arise and go to my father, and I will say to him, "Father, I have sinned against heaven and before you; I am no longer worthy to be called your son; treat me as one of your hired servants."' And he arose and came to his father.

179

"But while he was yet at a distance, his father saw him and had compassion, and ran and embraced him and kissed him. And the son said to him, 'Father, I have sinned against heaven and before you; I am no longer worthy to be called your son.' But the father said to his servants, 'Bring quickly the best robe, and put it on him; and put a ring on his hand, and shoes on his feet; and

bring the fatted calf and kill it, and let us eat and make merry; for this my son was dead, and is alive again; he was lost, and is found.' And they began to make merry.

"Now his elder son was in the field; and as he came and drew near to the house, he heard music and dancing. And he called one of the servants and asked what this meant. And he said to him, 'Your brother has come, and your father has killed the fatted calf, because he has received him safe and sound.' But he was angry and refused to go in. His father came out and entreated him, but he answered his father, 'Lo, these many years I have served you, and I never disobeyed your command; yet you never gave me a kid, that I might make merry with my friends. But when this son of yours came, who has devoured your living with harlots, you killed for him the fatted calf!' And the father said to him, 'Son, you are always with me, and all that is mine is yours. It was fitting to make merry and be glad, for this your brother was dead, and is alive; he was lost, and is found.' "

From Luke 15: 11–32.

A Grateful Foreigner

On the way to Jerusalem Jesus was passing along between Samar'ia and Galilee. And as he entered a village, he was met by ten lepers, who stood at a distance and lifted up their voices, "Jesus, Master, have mercy on us."

When Jesus saw them he said to them, "Go and show yourselves to the priests." And as they went they were cleansed. Then one of them, when he saw that he was healed, turned back, praising God with a loud voice; and he fell on his face at Jesus' feet, giving him thanks. Now he was a Samaritan.

Then said Jesus, "Were not ten cleansed? Where are the nine? Was no one found to return and give praise to God except this foreigner?" And he said to him, "Rise and go your way; your faith has made you well."

From Luke 17: 11–19.

Two Kinds of Prayer

Jesus also told this parable to some who trusted in themselves that they were righteous and despised others:

181

"Two men went up into the temple to pray, one a Pharisee and the other a tax collector. The Pharisee stood and prayed thus with himself, 'God, I thank thee that I am not like other men, extortioners, unjust, adulterers, or even like this tax collector. I fast twice a week, I give tithes of all that I get.' But the tax collector, standing far off, would not even lift up his eyes to heaven, but beat his breast, saying, 'God, be merciful to me a sinner!' I tell you, this man went down to his house justified rather than the other; for every one who exalts himself will be humbled, but he who humbles himself will be exalted."

From Luke 18: 9–14.

"Let the Children Come"

And they were bringing children to Jesus, that he might touch them; and the disciples rebuked them. But when Jesus saw it he was indignant, and said to them, "Let the children come to me, do not hinder them; for to such belongs the kingdom of God. Truly, I say to you, whoever does not receive the kingdom of God like a child shall not enter it." And he took them in his arms and blessed them, laying his hands upon them.

From Mark 10: 13–16.

"What Do I Lack?"

And behold, one came up to Jesus, saying, "Teacher, what good deed must I do, to have eternal life?"

And Jesus said to him, "Why do you ask me about what is good? One there is who is good. If you would enter life, keep the commandments."

He said to him, "Which?"

And Jesus said, "You shall not kill, You shall not commit adultery, You shall not steal, You shall not bear false witness, Honor your father and mother, and, You shall love your neighbor as yourself."

The young man said to him, "All these I have observed; what do I still lack?"

And Jesus looking upon him loved him, and said to him, "You lack one thing; go, sell what you have, and give to the poor, and you will have treasure in heaven; and come, follow me." At that saying the young man's countenance fell, and he went away sorrowful; for he had great possessions.

From Matthew 19: 16–20; Mark 10: 21–22; Luke 18: 24.

On the Road to Jerusalem

And the disciples were on the road, going up to Jerusalem, and Jesus was walking ahead of them; and they were amazed, and those who followed were afraid. And taking the twelve again, he began to tell them what was to happen to him, saying, "Behold, we are going up to Jerusalem; and the Son of man will be delivered to the chief priests and the scribes, and they will condemn him to death, and deliver him to the Gentiles; and they will mock him, and spit upon him, and scourge him, and kill him; and after three days he will rise."

And James and John, the sons of Zeb'edee, came forward, and said to Jesus, "Teacher, we want you to do for us whatever we ask of you."

And he said to them, "What do you want me to do for you?"

And they said to him, "Grant us to sit, one at your right hand and one at your left, in your glory."

But Jesus said to them, "You do not know what you are asking. Are you able to drink the cup that I drink, or to be baptized with the baptism with which I am baptized?"

And they said to him, "We are able."

And Jesus said to them, "The cup that I drink you will drink; and with the baptism with which I am baptized, you will be baptized; but to sit at my right hand or at my left is not mine to grant, but it is for those for whom it has been prepared."

And when the ten heard it, they began to be indignant at James and John. And Jesus called them to him and said to them, "You know that those who are supposed to rule over the Gentiles lord it over them, and their great men exercise authority over them. But it shall not be so among you; but whoever would be great among you must be your servant, and whoever would be first among you must be slave of all. For the Son of man also came not to be served but to serve, and to give his life as a ransom for many."

Jesus entered Jericho and was passing through. And there was a man named Zacchae'us; he was a chief tax collector, and rich. And he sought to see who Jesus was, but could not, on account of the crowd, because he was small of stature. So he ran on ahead and climbed up into a sycamore tree to see him, for he was to pass that way. And when Jesus came to the place, he looked up and said to him, "Zacchae'us, make haste and come down; for I must stay at your house today." So he made haste and came down, and received Jesus joyfully. And when the people saw it they all murmured, "He has gone in to be the guest of a man who is a sinner."

And Zacchae'us stood and said to the Lord, "Behold, Lord, the half of my goods I give to the poor; and if I have defrauded any one of anything, I restore it four-fold." And Jesus said to him, "Today salvation has come to this house, since he also is a son of Abraham. For the Son of man came to seek and to save the lost."

From Mark 10: 32–45; Luke 19: 1–10.

185

Jesus' Last Week in Jerusalem

And when they drew near to Jerusalem, to Beth'phage and Bethany, at the Mount of Olives, Jesus sent two of his disciples, and said to them, "Go into the village opposite you, and immediately as you enter it you will find a colt tied, on which no one has ever sat; untie it and bring it. If any one says to you, 'Why are you doing this?' say, 'The Lord has need of it and will send it back.'"

And they went away, and found a colt tied at the door out in the open street; and they untied it. And those who stood there said to them, "What are you doing, untying the colt?"

And they told them what Jesus had said; and they let them go. And they brought the colt to Jesus, and threw their garments on it; and he sat upon it.

And many spread their garments on the road, and others spread leafy branches which they had cut from the fields. And those who went before and those who followed cried out, "Hosanna! Blessed be he who comes in the name of the Lord! Blessed be the kingdom of our father David that is coming! Hosanna in the highest!"

186

And when he entered Jerusalem, all the city was stirred, saying, "Who is this?" And the crowds said, "This is the prophet Jesus from Nazareth of Galilee."

And Jesus entered the temple of God and drove out all who sold and bought in the temple, and he overturned the tables of the money-changers and the seats of those who sold pigeons. He said to them, "It is written, 'My house shall be called a house of prayer'; but you make it a den of robbers."

And the blind and the lame came to him in the temple, and he healed them. But when the chief priests and the scribes saw the wonderful things that he did, and the children crying out in the temple, "Hosanna to the Son of David!" they were indignant; and they said to him, "Do you hear what these are saying?"

And Jesus said to them, "Yes; have you never read,
'Out of the mouth of babes and sucklings
thou hast brought perfect praise'?"

And leaving them, he went out of the city to Bethany and lodged there.

And every day Jesus was teaching in the temple, but at night he went out and lodged on the mount called Olivet. And early in the morning all the people came to him in the temple to hear him.

One day, as he was teaching the people in the temple, Jesus looked up and saw the rich putting their gifts into the treasury; and he saw a poor widow put in two copper coins. And he said, "Truly I tell you, this poor widow has put in more than all of them; for they all contributed out of their abundance, but she out of her poverty put in all the living that she had."

From Mark 11: 1–10; Matthew 21: 10–17; Luke 21: 37–38; 20: 1; 21: 1–4.

Scribes and Pharisees Oppose Jesus

The scribes and the chief priests tried to lay hands on Jesus, but they feared the people. So they watched him, and sent spies, who pretended to be sincere, that they might take hold of what he said, so as to deliver him up to the authority and jurisdiction of the governor. They asked him, "Teacher, we know that you speak and teach rightly, and show no partiality, but teach the way of

188

God. Is it lawful for us to give tribute to Caesar, or not?"

But Jesus perceived their craftiness, and said to them, "Show me a coin. Whose likeness and inscription has it?"

They said, "Caesar's."

He said to them, "Then render to Caesar the things that are Caesar's, and to God the things that are God's." And they were not able in the presence of the people to catch him by what he said; but marveling at his answer they were silent.

And one of the scribes came up and heard them disputing with one another, and seeing that Jesus answered them well, asked, "Which commandment is the first?"

Jesus answered, "The first is, 'Hear, O Israel: The Lord our God, the Lord is one; and you shall love the Lord your God with all your heart, and with all your soul, and with all your mind, and with all your strength.' The second is this, 'You shall love your neighbor as yourself.' There is no other commandment greater than these."

And the scribe said to him, "You are right, Teacher; you have truly said that God is one, and there is no other but he; and to love him with all the heart, and with all the understanding, and with all the strength, and to love one's neighbor as oneself, is much more than all whole burnt offerings and sacrifices." And when Jesus saw that he answered wisely, he said to him, "You are not far from the kingdom of God." And after that no one dared to ask him any question.

Then said Jesus to the crowds and to his disciples, "The scribes and the Pharisees sit on Moses' seat; so

practice and observe whatever they tell you, but not what they do; for they preach, but do not practice. They bind heavy burdens, hard to bear, and lay them on men's shoulders; but they themselves will not move them with their finger. They do all their deeds to be seen by men; for they make their phylacteries broad and their fringes long, and they love the place of honor at feasts and the best seats in the synagogues, and salutations in the market places, and being called rabbi by men. But you are not to be called rabbi, for you have one teacher, and you are all brethren. And call no man your father on earth, for you have one Father, who is in heaven. Neither be called masters, for you have one master, the Christ. He who is greatest among you shall be your servant; whoever exalts himself will be humbled, and whoever humbles himself will be exalted.

"But woe to you, scribes and Pharisees, hypocrites! because you shut the kingdom of heaven against men; for you neither enter yourselves, nor allow those who would enter to go in.

"Woe to you, scribes and Pharisees, hypocrites! for you tithe mint and dill and cummin, and have neglected the weightier matters of the law, justice and mercy and faith; these you ought to have done, without neglecting the others. You blind guides, straining out a gnat and swallowing a camel!"

When Jesus had finished all these sayings, he said to his disciples, "You know that after two days the Passover is coming, and the Son of man will be delivered up to be crucified."

Then the chief priests and the elders of the people gathered in the palace of the high priest, who was called Ca'iaphas, and took counsel together in order to arrest Jesus by stealth and kill him. But they said, "Not during the feast, lest there be a tumult among the people."

From Luke 20: 19–26; Mark 12: 28–34; Matthew 23: 1–13, 23–24; 26: 1–5.

Anointing Jesus at Bethany

Now when Jesus was at Bethany in the house of Simon the leper, a woman came up to him with an alabaster jar of very expensive ointment, and she poured it on his head, as he sat at table. But when the disciples saw it, they were indignant, saying, "Why this waste? For this ointment might have been sold for a large sum, and given to the poor."

But Jesus, aware of this, said to them, "Why do you trouble the woman? For she has done a beautiful thing to me. For you always have the poor with you, but you will not always have me. In pouring this ointment on my body she has done it to prepare me for burial. Truly, I say to you, wherever this gospel is preached, what she has done will be told in memory of her."

Then one of the twelve, who was called Judas Iscariot, went to the chief priests and said, "What will you give me if I deliver him to you?" And they paid him thirty pieces of silver. And from that moment he sought an opportunity to betray Jesus.

From Matthew 26: 6–16.

The Last Supper

Now on the first day of Unleavened Bread the disciples came to Jesus, saying, "Where will you have us prepare for you to eat the passover?"

He said, "Go into the city to such a one, and say to him, 'The Teacher says, My time is at hand; I will keep the passover at your house with my disciples.'" And the disciples did as Jesus had directed them, and they prepared the passover.

Now before the feast of the Passover, Jesus, knowing that the Father had given all things into his hands, and that he had come from God and was going to God, rose from supper, laid aside his garments, and girded himself with a towel. Then he poured water into a basin, and began to wash the disciples' feet, and to wipe them with the towel with which he was girded.

When he had washed their feet, and taken his gar-

ments, and resumed his place, he said to them, "Do you know what I have done to you? You call me Teacher and Lord; and you are right, for so I am. If I then, your Lord and Teacher, have washed your feet, you also ought to wash one another's feet. For I have given you an example, that you also should do as I have done to you. Truly, truly, I say to you, a servant is not greater than his master; nor is he who is sent greater than he who sent him. If you know these things, blessed are you if you do them. Truly, truly, I say to you, he who receives any one whom I send receives me; and he who receives me receives him who sent me.

"I am the true vine, and my Father is the vinedresser. Every branch of mine that bears no fruit, he takes away, and every branch that does bear fruit he prunes, that it may bear more fruit. You are already made clean by the word which I have spoken to you. Abide in me, and I in you. As the branch cannot bear fruit by itself, unless

it abides in the vine, neither can you, unless you abide in me. I am the vine, you are the branches. He who abides in me, and I in him, he it is that bears much fruit, for apart from me you can do nothing.

"As the Father has loved me, so have I loved you; abide in my love. If you keep my commandments, you will abide in my love, just as I have kept my Father's commandments and abide in his love.

"This is my commandment, that you love one another as I have loved you. Greater love has no man than this, that a man lay down his life for his friends. You are my friends if you do what I command you. No longer do I call you servants, for the servant does not know what his master is doing; but I have called you friends, for all that I have heard from my Father I have made known to you."

And as they were eating, he said, "Truly, I say to you, one of you will betray me."

And they were very sorrowful, and began to say to him one after another, "Is it I, Lord?"

He answered, "He who has dipped his hand in the dish with me will betray me. The Son of man goes as it is written of him, but woe to that man by whom the Son of man is betrayed! It would have been better for that man if he had not been born."

Judas, who betrayed him, said, "Is it I, Master?"

He said to him, "You have said so."

Now as they were eating, Jesus took bread, and blessed, and broke it, and gave it to the disciples and said, "Take, eat; this is my body."

And he took a cup, and when he had given thanks he gave it to them, saying, "Drink of it, all of you; for this is my blood of the covenant, which is poured out for many for the forgiveness of sins."

From Matthew 26: 17–19; John 13: 1, 3–5, 12–17, 20; 15: 1–5, 9–10, 12–15; Matthew 26: 21–28.

Jesus Goes to Gethsemane

And when they had sung a hymn, they went out to the Mount of Olives.

Then Jesus said to the disciples, "You will all fall away because of me this night; for it is written, 'I will strike the shepherd, and the sheep of the flock will be scattered.' But after I am raised up, I will go before you to Galilee."

Peter declared to him, "Though they all fall away because of you, I will never fall away."

Jesus said to him, "Truly, I say to you, this very night, before the cock crows, you will deny me three times."

Peter said to him, "Even if I must die with you, I will not deny you." And so said all the disciples.

196

Then Jesus went with them to a place called Geth-sem'ane, and he said to his disciples, "Sit here, while I go yonder and pray."

And taking with him Peter and the two sons of Zeb'-edee, he began to be sorrowful and troubled. Then he said to them, "My soul is very sorrowful, even to death; remain here, and watch with me."

And going a little farther he fell on his face and prayed, "My Father, if it be possible, let this cup pass from me; nevertheless, not as I will, but as thou wilt."

And he came to the disciples and found them sleeping; and he said to Peter, "Could you not watch with me one hour? Watch and pray that you may not enter into temptation; the spirit indeed is willing, but the flesh is weak."

Again, for the second time, he went away and prayed, "My Father, if this cannot pass unless I drink it, thy will be done." And again he came and found them sleeping, for their eyes were heavy. So, leaving them again, he went away and prayed for the third time, saying the same words.

Then he came to the disciples and said to them, "Are you still sleeping and taking your rest? Behold, the hour is at hand, and the Son of man is betrayed into the hands of sinners. Rise, let us be going; my betrayer is at hand."

From Matthew 26: 30–46.

Judas Betrays Jesus

While Jesus was still speaking, Judas came, one of the twelve, and with him a great crowd with swords and clubs, from the chief priests and the elders of the people. Now the betrayer had given them a sign, saying, "The one I shall kiss is the man; seize him." And

he came up to Jesus at once and said, "Hail, Master!"
And he kissed him.

Jesus said to him, "Friend, why are you here?" Then
they came up and laid hands on Jesus and seized him.

And behold, one of those who were with Jesus
stretched out his hand and drew his sword, and struck
the slave of the high priest, and cut off his ear.

Jesus said to him, "Put your sword back into place; for
all who take the sword will perish by the sword."

At that hour Jesus said to the crowds, "Have you come
out as against a robber, with swords and clubs to cap-
ture me? Day after day I sat in the temple teaching, and
you did not seize me. But all this has taken place, that
the scriptures of the prophets might be fulfilled." Then
all the disciples forsook him and fled.

From Matthew 26: 47–52, 55–56.

And they led Jesus to the high priest; and all the chief priests and the elders and the scribes were assembled. And Peter had followed him at a distance, right into the courtyard of the high priest; and he was sitting with the guards, and warming himself at the fire.

Now the chief priests and the whole council sought testimony against Jesus to put him to death; but they found none. For many bore false witness against him, and their witness did not agree. And some stood up and bore false witness against him, saying, "We heard him say, 'I will destroy this temple that is made with hands, and in three days I will build another, not made with hands.'" Yet not even so did their testimony agree.

And the high priest stood up in the midst, and asked Jesus, "Have you no answer to make? What is it that these men testify against you?" But Jesus was silent.

Again the high priest asked him, "Are you the Christ, the Son of the Blessed?"

And Jesus said, "I am; and you will see the Son of man, sitting at the right hand of Power, and coming with the clouds of heaven."

And the high priest tore his mantle, and said, "Why do we still need witnesses? You have heard his blasphemy. What is your decision?" And they all condemned him as deserving death. And some began to spit on him, and to cover his face, and to strike him, saying to him, "Prophesy!" And the guards received him with blows.

And as Peter was below in the courtyard, one of the maids of the high priest came; and seeing Peter warming himself, she looked at him, and said, "You also were with the Nazarene, Jesus."

199

But he denied it, saying, "I neither know nor understand what you mean." And he went out into the gateway. And the maid saw him, and began again to say to the bystanders, "This man is one of them." But again he denied it. And after a little while again the bystanders said to Peter, "Certainly you are one of them; for you are a Galilean." But he began to swear, "I do not know this man of whom you speak."

And immediately the cock crowed a second time. And Peter remembered how Jesus had said to him, "Before the cock crows twice, you will deny me three times." And Peter broke down and wept.

When morning came, all the chief priests and the elders of the people took counsel against Jesus to put him to death. When Judas, his betrayer, saw that he was condemned, he repented and brought back the thirty pieces of silver to the chief priests and the elders, saying, "I have sinned in betraying innocent blood."

They said, "What is that to us? See to it yourself." And throwing down the pieces of silver in the temple, Judas departed; and he went and hanged himself.

From Mark 14: 53–72; Matthew 27: 1, 3–5.

Jesus Before Pilate

Then the whole company of them arose, and brought Jesus before Pilate. Pilate went out to them and said, "What accusation do you bring against this man?"

They answered him, "If this man were not an evildoer, we would not have handed him over." Pilate said, "Take him yourselves and judge him by your own law."

The Jews said to him, "It is not lawful for us to put any man to death."

Pilate entered the praetorium again and called Jesus, and said to him, "Are you the King of the Jews?"

Jesus answered, "Do you say this of your own accord, or did others say it to you about me?"

Pilate answered, "Am I a Jew? Your own nation and the chief priests have handed you over to me; what have you done?"

Jesus answered, "My kingship is not of this world; if my kingship were of this world, my servants would fight; but my kingship is not from the world."

Pilate said to him, "So you are a king?"

Jesus answered, "You say that I am a king. For this I was born, and for this I have come into the world, to bear witness to the truth. Every one who is of the truth hears my voice."

Pilate said to him, "What is truth?" After he had said this, he went out to the Jews again, and told them, "I find no crime in him. But you have a custom that I should release one man for you at the Passover; will you have me release for you the King of the Jews?"

They cried out again, "Not this man, but Barab'bas!" Now Barab'bas was a robber.

Then Pilate took Jesus and scourged him. And the

soldiers plaited a crown of thorns, and put it on his head, and arrayed him in a purple robe; they came up to him, saying, "Hail, King of the Jews!" and struck him with their hands.

Pilate went out again, and said to them, "Behold, I am bringing him out to you, that you may know that I find no crime in him." So Jesus came out, wearing the crown of thorns and the purple robe. Pilate said to them, "Here is the man!"

When the chief priests and the officers saw him, they cried out, "Crucify him, crucify him!"

Pilate said to them, "Take him yourselves and crucify him, for I find no crime in him."

The Jews answered him, "We have a law, and by that law he ought to die, because he has made himself the Son of God."

When Pilate heard these words, he was the more afraid; he entered the praetorium again and said to Jesus, "Where are you from?" But Jesus gave no answer. Pilate therefore said to him, "You will not speak to me? Do you know that I have power to release you, and power to crucify you?"

Jesus answered him, "You would have no power over
me unless it had been given you from above; therefore
he who delivered me to you has the greater sin."

Upon this Pilate sought to release him, but the Jews
cried out, "If you release this man, you are not Caesar's
friend; every one who makes himself a king sets himself
against Caesar." When Pilate heard these words, he
brought Jesus out and sat down on the judgment seat
at a place called The Pavement. Now it was the day of
Preparation for the Passover; it was about the sixth hour.
Pilate said to the Jews, "Here is your King!"

They cried out, "Away with him, away with him,
crucify him!"

Pilate said to them, "Shall I crucify your King?"

The chief priests answered, "We have no king but
Caesar."

So when Pilate saw that he was gaining nothing, but
rather that a riot was beginning, he took water and
washed his hands before the crowd, saying, "I am innocent of this man's blood; see to it yourselves."

And all the people answered, "His blood be on us and
on our children!" Then Pilate released for them Barab'-

bas, and having scourged Jesus, delivered him to be crucified.

From Luke 23: 1; John 18: 29–31, 33–40; 19: 1–15; Matthew 27: 24–26.

The Crucifixion

As they were marching out, they came upon a man of Cyre'ne, Simon by name; this man they compelled to carry his cross. And when they came to a place called Gol'gotha (which means the place of a skull), there they crucified him.

And Jesus said, "Father, forgive them; for they know not what they do." And they cast lots to divide his garments. Then they sat down and kept watch over him there. And over his head they put the charge against him, which read, "This is Jesus the King of the Jews."

Then two robbers were crucified with him, one on the right and one on the left. And those who passed by derided him, wagging their heads and saying, "You who would destroy the temple and build it in three days, save yourself! If you are the Son of God, come down from the cross." So also the chief priests, with the scribes and elders, mocked him, saying, "He saved others; he cannot save himself. He is the King of Israel; let him come down now from the cross, and we will believe in him. He trusts in God; let God deliver him now, if he desires him; for he said, 'I am the Son of God.'"

The soldiers also mocked him, coming up and offering him vinegar, and saying, "If you are the King of the Jews, save yourself!"

One of the criminals who were hanged railed at him, saying, "Are you not the Christ? Save yourself and us!"

But the other rebuked him, saying, "Do you not fear

God, since you are under the same sentence of condemnation? And we indeed justly; for we are receiving the due reward of our deeds; but this man has done nothing wrong." And he said, "Jesus, remember me when you come in your kingly power."

And Jesus said to him, "Truly, I say to you, today you will be with me in Paradise."

Now from the sixth hour there was darkness over all the land until the ninth hour. And about the ninth hour Jesus cried with a loud voice, "Eli, Eli, la'ma sabach-tha'ni?" that is, "My God, my God, why hast thou forsaken me?"

Standing by the cross of Jesus were his mother, and his mother's sister, Mary the wife of Clopas, and Mary Mag'dalene. When Jesus saw his mother, and the disciple whom he loved standing near, he said to his mother, "Woman, behold your son!" Then he said to the disciple, "Behold your mother!" And from that hour the disciple took her to his own home.

After this Jesus, knowing that all was now finished, said, "I thirst." A bowl full of vinegar stood there; so they put a sponge full of the vinegar on hyssop and held it to his mouth. When Jesus had received the vinegar, he said, "It is finished."

Then Jesus, crying with a loud voice, said, "Father, into thy hands I commit my spirit!" And having said this he breathed his last.

And when the centurion, who stood facing him, saw that he thus breathed his last, he said, "Truly this man was a son of God!"

From Matthew 27: 32–33; Luke 23: 33–34; Matthew 27: 36–43; Luke 23: 36–37, 39–43; Matthew 27: 45–46; John 19: 25–30; Luke 23: 46; Mark 15: 39.

The Empty Tomb

When it was evening, there came a rich man from Arimathe'a, named Joseph, who also was a disciple of Jesus. He went to Pilate and asked for the body of Jesus. Then Pilate ordered it to be given to him. And Joseph took the body, and wrapped it in a clean linen shroud, and laid it in his own new tomb, which he had hewn in the rock; and he rolled a great stone to the door of the tomb, and departed. Mary Mag'dalene and the other Mary were there, sitting opposite the sepulchre.

Next day, that is, after the day of Preparation, the chief priests and the Pharisees gathered before Pilate and said, "Sir, we remember how that impostor said, while he was still alive, 'After three days I will rise again.' Therefore order the sepulchre to be made secure until the third day, lest his disciples go and steal him away, and tell the people, 'He has risen from the dead,' and the last fraud will be worse than the first."

Pilate said to them, "You have a guard of soldiers; go,

make it as secure as you can." So they made the sepulchre secure by sealing the stone and setting a guard.

And when the sabbath was past, Mary Mag'dalene, Mary the mother of James, and Salo'me bought spices, so that they might go and anoint Jesus. And very early on the first day of the week they went to the tomb when the sun had risen. And they were saying to one another, "Who will roll away the stone for us from the door of the tomb?" And looking up, they saw that the stone was rolled back; for it was very large.

And entering the tomb, they saw a young man sitting on the right side, dressed in a white robe; and they were amazed. And he said to them, "Do not be amazed; you seek Jesus of Nazareth, who was crucified. He has risen, he is not here; see the place where they laid him. But go, tell his disciples and Peter that he is going before you to Galilee; there you will see him, as he told you."

From Matthew 27: 57–66; Mark 16: 1–7.

The Risen Christ

That very day two of the disciples were going to a village named Emma'us, about seven miles from Jerusalem, and talking with each other about all these things that had happened. While they were talking and discussing together, Jesus himself drew near and went with them. But their eyes were kept from recognizing him. And he said to them, "What is this conversation which you are holding with each other as you walk?" And they stood still, looking sad.

Then one of them, named Cle'opas, answered him, "Are you the only visitor to Jerusalem who does not know the things that have happened there in these days?"

And he said to them, "What things?"

208

And they said to him, "Concerning Jesus of Nazareth, who was a prophet mighty in deed and word before God and all the people, and how our chief priests and rulers delivered him up to be condemned to death, and crucified him. But we had hoped that he was the one to redeem Israel. Yes, and besides all this, it is now the third day since this happened. Moreover, some women of our company amazed us. They were at the tomb early in the morning and did not find his body; and they came back saying that they had even seen a vision of angels, who said that he was alive. Some of those who were with us went to the tomb, and found it just as the women had said; but him they did not see."

And he said to them, "O foolish men, and slow of heart to believe all that the prophets have spoken! Was it not necessary that the Christ should suffer these things and enter into his glory?" And beginning with Moses and all the prophets, he interpreted to them in all the scriptures the things concerning himself.

So they drew near to the village to which they were

going. He appeared to be going further, but they constrained him, saying, "Stay with us, for it is toward evening and the day is now far spent." So he went in to stay with them.

When he was at table with them, he took the bread and blessed, and broke it, and gave it to them. And their eyes were opened and they recognized him; and he vanished out of their sight.

They said to each other, "Did not our hearts burn within us while he talked to us on the road, while he opened to us the scriptures?" And they rose that same hour and returned to Jerusalem; and they found the eleven gathered together and those who were with them, who said, "The Lord has risen indeed, and has appeared to Simon!" Then they told what had happened on the road, and how he was known to them in the breaking of the bread.

After this Jesus revealed himself again to the disciples by the Sea of Tibe'ri-as. Jesus said to Simon Peter, "Simon, son of John, do you love me more than these?"

He said to him, "Yes, Lord; you know that I love you." Jesus said to him, "Feed my lambs."

A second time he said to him, "Simon, son of John, do you love me?" He said to him, "Yes, Lord; you know that I love you." Jesus said to him, "Tend my sheep."

He said to him the third time, "Simon, son of John, do you love me?" Peter was grieved because he said to him the third time, "Do you love me?" And he said to him, "Lord, you know everything; you know that I love you." Jesus said to him, "Feed my sheep." After this he said, "Follow me."

Now the eleven disciples went to Galilee, to the mountain to which Jesus had directed them. And when they saw him they worshiped him; but some doubted. And Jesus came and said to them, "All authority in heaven and on earth has been given to me. Go therefore and make disciples of all nations, baptizing them in the name of the Father and of the Son and of the Holy Spirit, teaching them to observe all that I have commanded you; and lo, I am with you always, to the close of the age."

From Luke 24: 13–35; John 21: 1, 15–17, 19; Matthew 28: 16–20.

The Meaning of Jesus' Life

In the beginning was the Word, and the Word was with God, and the Word was God. He was in the beginning with God; all things were made through him, and without him was not anything made that was made. In him was life, and the life was the light of men. The light shines in the darkness, and darkness has not overcome it.

The true light that enlightens every man was coming into the world. He was in the world, and the world was made through him, yet the world knew him not. He came to his own home, and his own people received him not. But to all who received him, who believed in his name, he gave power to become children of God.

And the Word became flesh and dwelt among us, full of grace and truth; we have beheld his glory, glory as of the only Son from the Father. For the law was given through Moses; grace and truth came through Jesus Christ. No one has ever seen God; the only Son, who is in the bosom of the Father, he has made him known.

For God so loved the world that he gave his only Son, that whoever believes in him should not perish but have eternal life.

From John 1: 1–5, 9–12, 14, 17–18; 3: 16.

211

Telling the Good News

The apostles returned to Jerusalem and went to the upper room where they were staying, Peter and John and James and Andrew, Philip and Thomas, Bartholomew and Matthew, James the son of Alphaeus and Simon the Zealot and Judas the son of James. All these with one accord devoted themselves to prayer, together with the women and Mary the mother of Jesus, and with his brothers.

When the day of Pentecost had come, they were all in one place. And suddenly a sound came from heaven like the rush of a mighty wind. And they were all filled with the Holy Spirit and began to speak in other tongues.

Now there were dwelling in Jerusalem Jews, devout men from every nation under heaven; and they were bewildered, because each one heard them speaking in his own language. And they said, "Are not all these who are speaking Galileans? And how is it that we hear them telling in our own tongues the mighty works of God?"

Then Peter addressed them, "Men of Israel, hear these words: Jesus of Nazareth, a man attested to you by God with mighty works and wonders and signs which God did through him, as you yourselves know—this Jesus, delivered up according to the definite plan and foreknowledge of God, you crucified and killed by the hands of lawless men. But God raised him up. Being therefore exalted at the right hand of God, and having received from the Father the promise of the Holy Spirit, he has poured out this which you see and hear. Let all the house of Israel therefore know that God has made him Lord and Christ, this Jesus whom you crucified."

Now when they heard this they were cut to the heart, and said to Peter and the rest of the apostles, "Brethren, what shall we do?"

And Peter said to them, "Repent, and be baptized in the name of Jesus Christ for the forgiveness of your sins; and you shall receive the gift of the Holy Spirit. For the promise is to you and to your children and to all that are far off, every one whom the Lord our God calls to him."

So those who received his word were baptized, and there were added that day about three thousand souls. And they devoted themselves to the apostles' teaching and fellowship.

And day by day, attending the temple together and breaking bread in their homes, they partook of food with glad and generous hearts, praising God and having favor with all the people. And the Lord added to their number day by day those who were being saved.

From Acts 1: 12–14; 2: 1–2, 4–8, 14, 22–24, 33, 36–39, 41–42, 46–47.

"We Must Obey God"

Now Peter and John were going up to the temple at the hour of prayer. And a man lame from birth was being

213

carried, whom they laid daily at that gate of the temple which is called Beautiful, to ask alms of those who entered the temple. Seeing Peter and John he asked for alms. And Peter directed his gaze at him, and said, "Look at us." And he fixed his attention upon them, expecting to receive something from them. But Peter said, "I have no silver and gold, but I give you what I have; in the name of Jesus Christ of Nazareth, walk." And he took him by the right hand and raised him up; and he stood and walked and entered the temple with them, walking and leaping and praising God. And all the people saw him and recognized him as the one who sat for alms at the Beautiful Gate; and they were filled with wonder and amazement at what had happened to him.

And Peter addressed the people, "Men of Israel, why do you wonder at this, or why do you stare at us, as though by our own power we had made him walk? The God of Abraham and Isaac and Jacob glorified his servant Jesus, whom you delivered up and denied in the presence of Pilate, when he decided to release him. But you asked for a murderer to be granted to you, and killed the Author of life, whom God raised from the dead. To this we are witnesses. And his name, by faith in his name, has made this man strong whom you see and know.

"And now, brethren, I know that you acted in ignorance, as did also your rulers. But what God foretold by the mouth of all the prophets, that his Christ should suffer, he thus fulfilled. Repent therefore, that your sins may be blotted out, that times of refreshing may come from the presence of the Lord."

And as they were speaking to the people, the priests and the captain of the temple and the Sad'ducees came upon them, annoyed because they were teaching the people and proclaiming in Jesus the resurrection from the dead. And they arrested Peter and John. But many of those who heard the word believed; and the number of the men came to about five thousand.

On the morrow the rulers and elders and scribes were gathered in Jerusalem, with Annas the high priest and Ca'iaphas. And when they had set them in the midst, they inquired, "By what power or by what name did you do this?" Then Peter, filled with the Holy Spirit, said to them, "Rulers of the people and elders, if we are being examined today concerning a good deed done to a cripple, be it known to you all, and to all the people of Israel, that by the name of Jesus Christ of Nazareth, whom you crucified, whom God raised from the dead, by him this man is standing before you well. And there is salvation in no one else, for there is no other name under heaven given among men by which we must be saved."

Now when they saw the boldness of Peter and John, and perceived that they were uneducated men, they wondered; and they recognized that they had been with Jesus. But seeing the man that had been healed standing beside them, they had nothing to say in opposition. But when they had commanded them to go aside out of the council, they conferred with one another, saying, "What shall we do with these men? For a notable sign has been performed and we cannot deny it. But in order that it may spread no further among the people, let us warn them to speak no more to any one in this name." So they called them and charged them not to speak or teach at all in the name of Jesus.

But Peter and John answered them, "Whether it is

right in the sight of God to listen to you rather than to God, you must judge; for we cannot but speak of what we have seen and heard." And when they had further threatened them, they let Peter and John go, finding no way to punish them, because of the people.

When Peter and John were released they went to their friends and reported what the chief priests and the elders had said to them. And when they heard it, they lifted their voices together to God and said, "Lord, look upon their threats, and grant to thy servants to speak thy word with all boldness." And when they had prayed, they were all filled with the Holy Spirit and spoke the word of God with boldness.

Now many signs and wonders were done among the people by the hands of the apostles. And they were all together in Solomon's Portico. And the people held them in high honor. And more than ever believers were added to the Lord, multitudes both of men and women.

But the high priest rose and all who were with him, and filled with jealousy, they arrested the apostles. And the high priest said to them, "We strictly charged you not to teach in this name, yet here you have filled Jerusalem with your teaching." But Peter and the apostles answered, "We must obey God rather than men."

When they heard this they were enraged and wanted to kill them. But a Pharisee named Gama'li-el, a teacher of the law, held in honor by all the people, stood up and ordered the men to be put outside for a while. And he said, "Men of Israel, take care what you do with these men; for if this plan or this undertaking is of men, it will fail; but if it is of God, you will not be able to overthrow them. You might even be found opposing God!"

So they took his advice, and when they had called in
the apostles, they beat them and charged them not to
speak in the name of Jesus, and let them go. Then they
left the presence of the council, rejoicing that they were
counted worthy to suffer dishonor for the name. And
every day in the temple and at home the apostles did
not cease teaching and preaching Jesus as the Christ.
From Acts 3: 1–19; 4: 1–10, 12–21, 23–24, 29, 31; 5: 12–14, 17–18, 27–29,
33–35, 38–42.

The Church Persecuted

Now when the disciples were increasing in numbers
the twelve summoned the body of disciples and said,
"It is not right that we should give up preaching to serve
tables. Therefore, pick out from among you seven men
of good repute whom we may appoint to this duty."

And they chose Stephen, a man full of faith and of the Holy Spirit, and six others.

And Stephen did great wonders and signs among the people. Then some of those who belonged to the synagogue disputed with Stephen. But they could not withstand the wisdom and the Spirit with which he spoke. Then they secretly instigated men, who said, "We have heard him speak blasphemous words against Moses and God." And they stirred up the people and the elders and the scribes, and they came upon him and seized him and brought him before the council, and set up false witnesses who said, "This man never ceases to speak words against this holy place and the law; for we have heard him say that this Jesus of Nazareth will destroy this place, and will change the customs which Moses delivered to us."

Now when they heard these things they were enraged, and they ground their teeth at him. But Stephen, full of the Holy Spirit, gazed into heaven and said, "Behold, I see the heavens opened, and the Son of man standing at the right hand of God." But they cried out with a loud voice and stopped their ears and rushed upon him. Then they cast him out of the city and stoned him. And the witnesses laid down their garments at the feet of a young man named Saul.

And as they were stoning Stephen, he prayed, "Lord Jesus, receive my spirit." And he knelt down and cried with a loud voice, "Lord, do not hold this sin against them." And when he had said this, he died. And Saul was consenting to his death.

And on that day a great persecution arose against the church in Jerusalem; and they were all scattered throughout the region of Judea and Samar'ia, except the apostles. Devout men buried Stephen, and made great lamentation over him. But Saul laid waste the church, and entering house after house, he dragged off men and women and committed them to prison. Now those who were scattered went about preaching the word.

From Acts 6: 1–3, 5, 8–14; 7: 54–60; 8: 1–4.

The Conversion of Saul

But Saul, still breathing threats and murder against the disciples of the Lord, went to the high priest and asked him for letters to the synagogues at Damascus, so that if he found any belonging to the Way, men or women, he might bring them bound to Jerusalem. Now as he journeyed he approached Damascus, and suddenly a light from heaven flashed about him. And he fell to the ground and heard a voice saying to him, "Saul, Saul, why do you persecute me?" And he said, "Who are you, Lord?" He said, "I am Jesus, whom you are persecuting; but rise and enter the city, and you will be told what you are to do." The men who were traveling with him stood speechless, hearing the voice but seeing no one. Saul arose from the ground; and he could see nothing; so they led him by the hand and brought him into Damascus. And for three days he was without sight, and neither ate nor drank.

Now there was a disciple at Damascus named Anani'as. The Lord said to him in a vision, "Anani'as, rise and go to the street called Straight, and inquire in the house of Judas for a man named Saul." But Anani'as answered, "Lord, I have heard from many about this man, how much evil he has done to thy saints at Jerusalem; and here he has authority from the chief priests to bind all who call upon thy name." But the Lord said, "Go, for he is a chosen instrument of mine to carry my name before the Gentiles; for I will show him how much he must suffer for the sake of my name."

So Anani'as departed and entered the house. And laying his hands on him he said, "Brother Saul, the Lord Jesus, who appeared to you on the road by which you came, has sent me that you may regain your sight and be filled with the Holy Spirit." And immediately Saul regained his sight. Then he rose and was baptized, and took food and was strengthened.

For several days Saul was with the disciples at Damascus. And in the synagogues he proclaimed Jesus, saying, "He is the Son of God." And all who heard him were amazed, and said, "Is not this the man who made havoc in Jerusalem of those who called on this name? And he has come here for this purpose, to bring them bound before the chief priests." But Saul increased all the more in strength, and confounded the Jews who lived in Damascus by proving that Jesus was the Christ.

When many days had passed, the Jews plotted to kill him, but their plot became known to Saul. And friends took him by night and let him down over the wall, lowering him in a basket.

When Saul had come to Jerusalem he attempted to join the disciples; and they were all afraid of him. But Barnabas brought him to the apostles, and declared to them how on the road Saul had seen the Lord, who spoke to him, and how at Damascus he had preached boldly in the name of Jesus. So he went in and out among them at Jerusalem, preaching boldly in the name of the Lord.

From Acts 9: 1–11, 13–29.

Peter and the Gentiles

At Caesare'a there was a man named Cornelius, a centurion of the Italian Cohort, a devout man who feared God, gave alms liberally to the people, and prayed constantly to God. He saw clearly in a vision an angel of God who said to him, "Your prayers and your alms have ascended as a memorial before God. Now send men to Joppa, and bring one Simon who is called Peter; he is lodging with Simon, a tanner, whose house is by the seaside." When the angel had departed, Cornelius called his servants and a devout soldier, and having related everything to them, sent them to Joppa.

The men that were sent by Cornelius, having made inquiry for Simon's house, stood before the gate and called out to ask whether Peter was lodging there. And Peter went down and said, "I am the one you are looking for; what is the reason for your coming?" And they said, "Cornelius, a centurion, an upright and God-fearing man, who is well spoken of by the whole Jewish nation, was directed by an angel to send for you to come to his house, and to hear what you have to say."

The next day Peter went with them, and some of the brethren from Joppa accompanied him. And on the following day they entered Caesare'a. Cornelius was expecting them and had called together his kinsmen and close friends. When Peter entered, he found many persons gathered; and he said to them, "You know how unlawful it is for a Jew to associate with or to visit any one of another nation; but God has shown me that I should not call any man common or unclean. So when I was sent for, I came without objection."

And Cornelius said, "We are all here present in the

sight of God, to hear what you have been commanded by the Lord."

And Peter said: "Truly I perceive that God shows no partiality, but in every nation any one who fears him and does what is right is acceptable to him. You know the word which he sent to Israel, preaching good news of peace by Jesus Christ. He is Lord of all. And we are witnesses to all that he did."

While Peter was still saying this, the Holy Spirit fell on all who heard the word. And the believers who came with Peter were amazed, because the gift of the Holy Spirit had been poured out even on the Gentiles. Then Peter commanded them to be baptized in the name of Jesus Christ.

Now the apostles and the brethren who were in Judea heard that the Gentiles also had received the word of God. So when Peter went up to Jerusalem, the circumcision party criticized him, saying, "Why did you go to uncircumcised men and eat with them?" But Peter began and explained to them what had happened in the city of Joppa. When they heard this they were silenced. And they glorified God, saying, "Then to the Gentiles also God has granted repentance unto life."

From Acts 10: 1–8, 17–18, 21–25, 27–30, 33–36, 39, 44–46, 48; 11: 1–5, 18.

The Christians at Antioch

Now those who were scattered because of the persecution that arose over Stephen traveled as far as Phoeni'cia and Cyprus and Antioch, speaking the word to none except Jews. But there were some of them who on coming to Antioch spoke to the Greeks also, preaching the Lord Jesus. And a great number that believed turned

223

to the Lord. News of this came to the church in Jerusalem, and they sent Barnabas to Antioch. When he came and saw the grace of God, he was glad; and he exhorted them all to remain faithful to the Lord with steadfast purpose. And Barnabas went to Tarsus to look for Saul; and when he had found him, he brought him to Antioch. For a whole year they met with the church, and taught a large company of people; and in Antioch the disciples were for the first time called Christians.

Now prophets came down from Jerusalem to Antioch and foretold by the Spirit that there would be a great famine. And the disciples determined, every one according to his ability, to send relief to the brethren who lived in Judea; and they did so, sending it to the elders by the hand of Barnabas and Saul.

And they returned from Jerusalem when they had fulfilled their mission.

Now in the church at Antioch, while they were worshiping the Lord and fasting, the Holy Spirit said, "Set apart for me Barnabas and Saul for the work to which I have called them." Then they laid their hands on them and sent them off.

When they arrived at Sal'amis, they proclaimed the word of God in the synagogues of the Jews.

From Acts 11: 19–23, 25–30; 12: 25; 13: 1–3, 5.

Paul's Mission to the Gentiles

Now Saul, who is also called Paul, and his company came to Antioch of Pisid'ia. And on the sabbath day they went into the synagogue and sat down. After the reading of the law and the prophets, the rulers of the synagogue sent to them, saying, "Brethren, if you have any word of exhortation for the people, say it." So Paul

stood up, and said: "Brethren, sons of the family of Abraham, and those among you that fear God, to us has been sent the message of this salvation. And we bring you the good news that what God promised to the fathers, this he has fulfilled to us their children by raising Jesus. Let it be known to you therefore, brethren, that through this man forgiveness of sins is proclaimed to you, and by him every one that believes is freed from everything from which you could not be freed by the law of Moses."

As they went out, the people begged that these things might be told them the next sabbath.

The next sabbath almost the whole city gathered together to hear the word of God. But when the Jews saw the multitudes, they were filled with jealousy, and contradicted what was spoken by Paul, and reviled him. And Paul and Barnabas spoke out boldly, saying, "It was necessary that the word of God should be spoken first to you. Since you thrust it from you, and judge yourselves unworthy of eternal life, behold, we turn to the Gentiles. For so the Lord has commanded us, saying,

'I have set you to be a light for the Gentiles,
that you may bring salvation to the uttermost parts
of the earth.' "

225

And when the Gentiles heard this, they were glad and glorified the word of God. And the word of the Lord spread throughout all the region.

Now at Ico'nium Paul and Barnabas entered into the Jewish synagogue, and so spoke that a great company believed, both of Jews and Greeks. But the unbelieving Jews stirred up the Gentiles and poisoned their minds against them. When an attempt was made to molest Paul and Barnabas they fled to Lystra and Derbe, and there they preached the gospel.

But Jews came there from Antioch and Ico'nium; and having persuaded the people, they stoned Paul and dragged him out of the city, supposing that he was dead. But when the disciples gathered about him, he rose up and entered the city; and on the next day he went on with Barnabas to Derbe. When they had preached the gospel to that city and had made many disciples, they returned to Lystra and to Ico'nium and to Antioch. And they appointed elders in every church, and committed them to the Lord in whom they believed.

From Acts 13: 9, 13–16, 26, 32–33, 38–39, 42, 44–49; 14: 1–2, 5–7, 19–21, 23.

The Church Accepts Gentiles

But some men came down from Judea and were teaching the brethren, "Unless you are circumcised according to the custom of Moses, you cannot be saved." And when Paul and Barnabas had no small dissension and debate with them, Paul and Barnabas and some of the others were appointed to go up to Jerusalem to the apostles and the elders about this question. When they came to Jerusalem, they were welcomed by the church and the apostles and the elders, and they declared all that God had done. But some believers who belonged to the party of the Pharisees said, "It is necessary to circumcise the Gentiles and to charge them to keep the law of Moses."

The apostles and the elders were gathered to consider this matter. And after much debate, Peter rose and said to them, "Brethren, you know that in the early days God made choice among you, that by my mouth the Gentiles should hear the word of the gospel and believe. And God who knows the heart bore witness to them, giving them the Holy Spirit just as he did to us; and he made no distinction between us and them, but cleansed their hearts by faith. Now why do you make trial of God by putting a yoke upon their neck which neither our fathers nor we have been able to bear? But we believe that we shall be saved through the grace of the Lord Jesus, just as they will."

And all the assembly kept silence; and they listened to Barnabas and Paul as they related what signs and wonders God had done through them among the Gentiles. After they finished speaking, James replied, "Brethren, listen to me. Peter has related how God first visited the Gentiles, to take out of them a people for his name. And with this the words of the prophets agree. Therefore my judgment is that we should not trouble those of the Gentiles who turn to God, but should write to them to abstain from the pollutions of idols and from unchastity and from what is strangled and from blood."

Then it seemed good to the apostles and the elders, with the whole church, to choose men and send them to Antioch with Paul and Barnabas. They sent Judas and Silas with the following letter: "The brethren, both the apostles and the elders, to the brethren who are of the

Gentiles in Antioch and Syria and Cili'cia, greeting. Since we have heard that some persons from us have troubled you with words, unsettling your minds, although we gave them no instructions, it has seemed good to us in assembly to choose men and send them to you with our beloved Barnabas and Paul, men who have risked their lives for the sake of our Lord Jesus Christ. We have therefore sent Judas and Silas, who themselves will tell you the same things by word of mouth. For it has seemed good to the Holy Spirit and to us to lay upon you no greater burden than these necessary things: that you abstain from what has been sacrificed to idols and from blood and from what is strangled and from unchastity. If you keep yourselves from these, you will do well. Farewell."

So when they were sent off, they went to Antioch; and having gathered the congregation together, they delivered the letter. And when they read it, they rejoiced at the exhortation.

From Acts 15: 1-2, 4-15, 19-20, 22-31.

Paul's Mission to Europe

Paul and his companions went to Troas, and a vision appeared to Paul in the night: a man of Macedo'nia was beseeching him and saying, "Come over to Macedo'nia and help us." And when he had seen the vision, immediately we sought to go on into Macedo'nia, concluding that God had called us to preach the gospel to them.

Setting sail therefore from Tro'as, we went to Philippi, which is the leading city of the district of Macedo'nia, and a Roman colony. We remained in this city some days; and on the sabbath day we went outside the gate

to the riverside, where we supposed there was a place of prayer; and we sat down and spoke to the women who had come together. One who heard us was a woman named Lydia, a seller of purple goods, who was a worshiper of God. The Lord opened her heart to give heed to what was said by Paul. And when she was baptized, with her household, she besought us, saying, "If you have judged me to be faithful to the Lord, come to my house and stay." And she prevailed upon us.

As we were going to the place of prayer, we were met by a slave girl who had a spirit of divination and brought her owners much gain by soothsaying. She followed Paul and us, crying, "These men are servants of the Most High God, who proclaim to you the way of salvation." Paul said to the spirit, "I charge you in the name of Jesus Christ to come out of her." And it came out.

But when her owners saw that their hope of gain was gone, they seized Paul and Silas and dragged them into the market place before the magistrates and said, "These men are Jews and they are disturbing our city. They advocate customs which it is not lawful for us Romans to accept or practice." The crowd joined in attacking them; and the magistrates tore the garments off them and gave orders to beat them. And they threw them into prison, charging the jailer to keep them safely. He put them into the inner prison and fastened their feet in the stocks.

But about midnight Paul and Silas were praying and singing hymns to God, and the prisoners were listening to them, and suddenly there was a great earthquake, so that the foundations of the prison were shaken; and all the doors were opened and every one's fetters were unfastened. When the jailer woke and saw that the prison doors were open, he drew his sword and was about to kill himself, supposing that the prisoners had escaped. But Paul cried with a loud voice, "Do not harm yourself, for we are all here."

The jailer called for lights and rushed in, and trembling with fear he fell down before Paul and Silas, and brought them out and said, "Men, what must I do to be saved?" And they said, "Believe in the Lord Jesus, and you will be saved, you and your household." And they spoke the word of the Lord to him and to all that were in the house. And he took them and washed their wounds, and he was baptized at once, with all his family. Then he brought them up into his house, and set food before them; and he rejoiced with all his household that he had believed in God.

But when it was day, the magistrates sent the police, saying, "Let those men go." And the jailer reported the words to Paul, saying, "The magistrates have sent to let you go; now come out and go in peace." But Paul said to them, "They have beaten us publicly, uncondemned, men who are Roman citizens, and have thrown us into prison; and do they now cast us out secretly? No! let them come themselves and take us out." The police reported these words to the magistrates, and they were

afraid when they heard that they were Roman citizens;
so they came and apologized to them. And they took
them out and asked them to leave the city. So they went
out of the prison, and visited Lydia; and when they had
seen the brethren, they exhorted them and departed.

Paul went to Corinth. And he found a Jew named
Aquila, lately come from Italy with his wife Priscilla,
because Claudius had commanded all the Jews to leave
Rome. And he went to see them; and because he was of
the same trade he stayed with them, and they worked,
for they were tentmakers. And in the synagogue every
sabbath, he persuaded Jews and Greeks. And he stayed
a year and six months, teaching the word of God.

Paul came to Ephesus where he found some disciples.
And he entered the synagogue and spoke, boldly, argu-
ing and pleading about the kingdom of God. Later he
withdrew and argued daily in the hall of Tyran'nus. This
continued for two years, so that all the people heard the
word of the Lord, both Jews and Greeks.

Then Paul called to him the elders of the church at
Ephesus and said to them: "You know how I lived among
you all the time from the first day that I set foot in Asia,
serving the Lord with all humility. And now I am going
to Jerusalem, not knowing what shall befall me there.
I commend you to God and to the word of his grace,
which is able to build you up."

When he had spoken thus, he knelt down and prayed
with them. And they all wept and embraced Paul, sor-
rowing because of the word he had spoken, that they
should see his face no more. And they brought him to
the ship.

From Acts 16: 8–40; 18: 1–4, 11; 19: 1, 8–10; 20: 1, 17–19, 22, 32, 36–38.

"A Pestilent Fellow"

When we had come to Jerusalem, the brethren received us gladly. On the following day Paul went with us to James; and all the elders were present. After greeting them, he related the things that God had done among the Gentiles through his ministry. And when they heard it, they glorified God.

The next day Paul purified himself and went into the temple. Some Jews saw him in the temple and laid hands on him, crying out, "Men of Israel, help! This is the man who is teaching men everywhere against the law and this place; moreover he also brought Greeks into the temple, and he has defiled this holy place." For they had previously seen Troph'imus the Ephesian with him in the city, and they supposed that Paul had brought him into the temple. Then all the city was aroused, and the people ran together; they seized Paul and dragged him out of the temple. And as they were trying to kill him, word came to the tribune that all Jerusalem was in confusion. He at once took soldiers and centurions, and ran

down to them; and when they saw the tribune and the soldiers, they stopped beating Paul. Then the tribune came up and arrested him.

As Paul was about to be brought into the barracks, he said to the tribune, "May I say something to you?" And the tribune said, "Do you know Greek? Are you not the Egyptian who recently stirred up a revolt and led four thousand Assassins into the wilderness?" Paul replied, "I am a Jew, from Tarsus, a citizen of no mean city."

As the people were crying out and waving their garments and throwing dust into the air, the tribune commanded Paul to be brought into the barracks, and ordered him to be examined by scourging, to find out why they shouted thus against him. But when they had tied him up with the thongs, Paul said to the centurion, "Is it lawful for you to scourge a man who is a Roman citizen, and uncondemned?"

When the centurion heard that, he went to the tribune and said to him, "What are you about to do? For this man is a Roman citizen." So the tribune came and said to him, "Tell me, are you a Roman citizen?" And he said, "Yes." The tribune answered, "I bought this citizenship for a large sum." Paul said, "But I was born a citizen." So those who were about to examine him withdrew from him; and the tribune was afraid, for he realized that Paul was a Roman citizen and that he had bound him.

But on the morrow, desiring to know the real reason why the Jews accused him, he unbound him, and commanded the chief priests and all the council to meet, and he brought Paul down and set him before them.

And Paul, looking intently at the council, said, "Brethren, I have lived before God in all good conscience up to this day." And the high priest Anani'as commanded those who stood by him to strike him on the mouth.

Then a great clamor arose; and some of the scribes of the Pharisees' party stood up and contended, "We find nothing wrong in this man." And when the dissension became violent, the tribune, afraid that Paul would be torn in pieces by them, commanded the soldiers to go down and take him by force from among them and bring him into the barracks.

The following night the Lord stood by him and said, "Take courage, for as you have testified about me at Jerusalem, so you must bear witness also at Rome."

When it was day, some Jews made a plot and bound themselves by an oath neither to eat nor drink till they had killed Paul. And they went to the chief priests and elders, and said, "We have strictly bound ourselves by an oath to taste no food till we have killed Paul. Give notice now to the tribune to bring him down to you, as though you were going to determine his case more exactly. We are ready to kill him before he comes."

Now the son of Paul's sister heard of their ambush; so he went to the barracks and told Paul. And Paul called one of the centurions and said, "Bring this young man to the tribune; for he has something to tell him." So he took him to the tribune. The tribune charged him, "Tell no one that you have informed me of this."

Then he called two of the centurions and said, "At the third hour of the night get ready two hundred soldiers with seventy horsemen and two hundred spearmen to go as far as Caesare'a. Also provide mounts for Paul to ride, and bring him safely to Felix the governor." And he wrote a letter to the governor Felix.

So the soldiers took Paul. When they came to Caesare'a and delivered the letter to the governor, they presented Paul also before him. On reading the letter, Felix said, "I will hear you when your accusers arrive." And he commanded him to be guarded in Herod's praetorium.

After five days the high priest Anani'as came down with some elders and a spokesman. They laid before the governor their case against Paul. "We have found this man a pestilent fellow, an agitator among all the Jews throughout the world, and a ringleader of the sect of the Nazarenes. He even tried to profane the temple, but we seized him. By examining him you will be able to learn about everything of which we accuse him."

And when the governor had motioned to him to speak, Paul replied: "Since for many years you have been judge over this nation, I cheerfully make my defense."

As Paul argued about justice and self-control and future judgment, Felix was alarmed and said, "Go away for the present; when I have an opportunity I will summon you." At the same time he hoped that money would be given him by Paul. So he sent for him often and conversed with him. When two years had elapsed, Felix was succeeded by Festus.

Festus took his seat on the tribunal and ordered Paul to be brought. And when he had come, the Jews who had gone down from Jerusalem stood about him, bringing against him many serious charges which they could not prove. Paul said in his defense, "Neither against the law of the Jews, nor against the temple, nor against Caesar have I offended at all."

But Festus, wishing to do the Jews a favor, said to Paul, "Do you wish to go up to Jerusalem, and there be tried on these charges before me?" But Paul said, "I am standing before Caesar's tribunal, where I ought to be tried; to the Jews I have done no wrong, as you know very well. If then I am a wrongdoer, and have committed anything for which I deserve to die, I do not seek to escape death; but if there is nothing in their charges against me, no one can give me up to them. I appeal to Caesar." Then Festus, when he had conferred with his council, answered, "You have appealed to Caesar; to Caesar you shall go."

From Acts 21: 17–20, 26–33, 37–39; 22: 23–30; 23: 1–2, 9–12, 14–18, 22–25, 31, 33–35; 24: 1, 5–6, 8, 10, 25–27; 25: 6–12.

Paul Pleads His Case

Now when some days had passed, Agrippa the king and Bernice arrived at Caesare'a to welcome Festus. And Festus laid Paul's case before the king, saying, "There is a man left prisoner by Felix; but I have nothing definite to write to Caesar about him. Therefore I have brought him before you, King Agrippa, that, after we have examined him, I may have something to write. For it seems to me unreasonable, in sending a prisoner, not to indicate the charges against him."

So on the morrow Agrippa and Bernice came with great pomp, and they entered the audience hall. Then by command of Festus, Paul was brought in.

Agrippa said to Paul, "You have permission to speak for yourself." Then Paul made his defense:

"I think myself fortunate that it is before you, King Agrippa, I am to make my defense today against all the accusations of the Jews, because you are especially familiar with all customs and controversies of the Jews; therefore I beg you to listen to me patiently.

"My manner of life from my youth, spent from the beginning among my own nation and at Jerusalem, is known by all the Jews. They have known for a long time, if they are willing to testify, that according to the strictest party of our religion I have lived as a Pharisee. And now I stand here on trial for hope in the promise made by God to our fathers.

"I myself was convinced that I ought to do many things in opposing the name of Jesus of Nazareth. And I did so in Jerusalem; I not only shut up many of the saints in prison, by authority from the chief priests, but when they were put to death I cast my vote against them. And I punished them often in all the synagogues and tried to make them blaspheme; and in raging fury against them, I persecuted them even to foreign cities.

"Thus I journeyed to Damascus with the authority and commission of the chief priests. At midday, O king, I saw on the way a light from heaven, brighter than the sun, shining round me and those who journeyed with me. And when we had fallen to the ground, I heard a voice saying to me in the Hebrew language, 'Saul, Saul, why do you persecute me? It hurts you to kick against the goads.' And I said, 'Who are you, Lord?' And the Lord said, 'I am Jesus whom you are persecuting. But rise and stand upon your feet; for I have appeared to you to appoint you to serve and bear witness to those to whom I send you, that they may turn from darkness to light and from the power of Satan to God, that they may receive forgiveness of sins and a place among those who are sanctified by faith in me.'

"Wherefore, O King Agrippa, I was not disobedient to the heavenly vision, but declared first to those at Damascus, then at Jerusalem and throughout all the country of Judea, and also to the Gentiles, that they should repent and turn to God and perform deeds worthy of their repentance. For this reason the Jews seized me in the temple and tried to kill me. To this day I have had the help that comes from God, and so I stand here testifying both to small and great, saying nothing but what the prophets and Moses said would come to pass: that the Christ must suffer, and that, by being the first to rise from the dead, he would proclaim light both to the people and to the Gentiles."

And Agrippa said to Paul, "In a short time you think to make me a Christian!" And Paul said, "Whether short or long, I would to God that not only you but also all who hear me this day might become such as I am— except for these chains."

Then the king rose, and the governor and Bernice and those who were sitting with them; and when they had withdrawn, they said to one another, "This man is doing nothing to deserve death or imprisonment." And

Agrippa said to Festus, "This man could have been set free if he had not appealed to Caesar."

And when it was decided that we should sail for Italy, they delivered Paul and some other prisoners to a centurion named Julius. And embarking in a ship which was about to sail along the coast of Asia, we put to sea.

From Acts 25: 13–14, 26–27, 23; 26: 1–6, 9–16, 18–23, 28–32; 27: 1–2.

Shipwreck

A tempestuous wind, called the northeaster, struck down from the land; and when the ship was caught and could not face the wind, we gave way to it and were driven. As we were violently storm-tossed, they began next day to throw the cargo overboard; and the third day they cast out the tackle of the ship.

When neither sun nor stars appeared for many a day, all hope of our being saved was abandoned.

Paul then came forward and said, "I bid you take heart; for there will be no loss of life among you, but only of the ship. This very night there stood by me an angel of the God to whom I belong and whom I worship, and he said, 'Do not be afraid, Paul; you must stand before

239

Caesar; and God has granted you all those who sail with
you.' So take heart, men, for I have faith in God that it
will be exactly as I have been told. But we shall have to
run on some island."

When the fourteenth night had come, as we were
drifting across the sea, about midnight the sailors sus-
pected that they were nearing land.

Now when it was day, they did not recognize the
land, but they noticed a bay with a beach, on which they
planned if possible to bring the ship ashore. So they cast
off the anchors and left them in the sea, at the same time
loosening the ropes that tied the rudders; then hoisting
the foresail to the wind they made for the beach. But
striking a shoal they ran the vessel aground; the bow
stuck and remained immovable, and the stern was
broken up by the surf. The centurion ordered those who
could swim to throw themselves overboard first and
make for the land, and the rest on planks or on pieces of
the ship. And so all escaped to land.

After we had escaped, we learned that the island was
called Malta. And the natives showed us unusual kindness, for they kindled a fire and welcomed us all, because
it had begun to rain and was cold.

After three months we set sail in a ship which had
wintered in the island, a ship of Alexandria, with the
Twin Brothers as figurehead.

From Acts 27: 14–15, 18–27, 39–41, 43–44; 28: 1–2, 11.

Paul at Rome

And so we came to Rome. And the brethren there,
when they heard of us, came as far as the Forum of
Ap'pius to meet us. On seeing them Paul thanked God

and took courage. And when we came into Rome, Paul was allowed to stay by himself, with the soldier that guarded him.

After three days Paul called together the local leaders of the Jews; and when they had gathered, he said to them, "Brethren, though I had done nothing against the people or the customs of our fathers, yet I was delivered prisoner from Jerusalem into the hands of the Romans. When they had examined me, they wished to set me at liberty, because there was no reason for the death penalty in my case. But when the Jews objected, I was compelled to appeal to Caesar—though I had no charge to bring against my nation. For this reason therefore I have asked to see you and speak with you, since it is because of the hope of Israel that I am bound with this chain."

And they said to him, "We have received no letters from Judea about you, and none of the brethren coming here has reported any evil about you. But we desire to hear from you what your views are; for with regard to this sect we know that everywhere it is spoken against."

When they had appointed a day for him, they came to Paul at his lodging in great numbers. And he expounded the matter to them from morning till evening, testifying to the kingdom of God and trying to convince them about Jesus both from the law of Moses and from the prophets. And some were convinced by what he said, while others disbelieved.

And he lived there two whole years at his own expense, and welcomed all who came to him, preaching the kingdom of God and teaching about the Lord Jesus Christ quite openly and unhindered.

From Acts 28: 14–24, 30–31.

Letters to the Churches

From Paul to the Romans

From Paul, a servant of Jesus Christ, called to be an apostle, to all God's beloved in Rome, who are called to be saints:

First, I thank my God through Jesus Christ for all of you, because your faith is proclaimed in all the world. For God is my witness, that without ceasing I mention you always in my prayers, asking that somehow by God's will I may now at last succeed in coming to you. I long to see you, for I am eager to preach the gospel to you also who are in Rome.

For I am not ashamed of the gospel: it is the power of God for salvation to every one who has faith, to the Jew first and also to the Greek. For in it the righteousness of God is revealed through faith for faith; as it is written, "He who through faith is righteous shall live."

We know that in everything God works for good with those who love him, who are called according to his purpose. If God is for us, who is against us? Who shall separate us from the love of Christ? Shall tribulation, or distress, or persecution, or famine, or nakedness, or peril, or sword? No, in all these things we are more than conquerors through him who loved us. For I am sure that neither death, nor life, nor angels, nor principalities, nor things present, nor things to come, nor powers, nor height, nor depth, nor anything else in all creation, will be able to separate us from the love of God in Christ Jesus our Lord.

I appeal to you, brethren, by the mercies of God, to present your bodies as a living sacrifice, holy and acceptable to God, which is your spiritual worship. Do not be conformed to this world but be transformed by the renewal of your mind, that you may prove what is the will of God, what is good and acceptable and perfect.

For by the grace given to me I bid every one among you not to think of himself more highly than he ought to think, but to think with sober judgment, each according to the measure of faith which God has assigned him. For as in one body we have many members, and all the members do not have the same function, so we, though many, are one body in Christ, and individually members one of another. Having gifts that differ according to the grace given to us, let us use them: if prophecy, in proportion to our faith; if service, in our serving; he who teaches, in his teaching; he who exhorts, in his exhortation; he who contributes, in liberality; he who gives aid, with zeal; he who does acts of mercy, with cheerfulness.

Let love be genuine; hate what is evil, hold fast to what is good; love one another with brotherly affection; outdo one another in showing honor. Never flag in zeal, be aglow with the Spirit, serve the Lord. Rejoice in your hope, be patient in tribulation, be constant in prayer. Contribute to the needs of the saints, practice hospitality.

Bless those who persecute you; bless and do not curse them. Rejoice with those who rejoice, weep with those who weep. Live in harmony with one another; do not be haughty, but associate with the lowly; never be conceited. Repay no one evil for evil, but take thought for what is noble in the sight of all. If possible, so far as it depends upon you, live peaceably with all. If your enemy is hungry, feed him; if he is thirsty, give him drink; for by so doing you will heap burning coals upon his head. Do not be overcome by evil, but overcome evil with good.

From Romans 1: 1, 7–11, 15–17; 8: 28, 31, 35, 37–39; 12: 1–18, 20–21.

From Paul to the Corinthians

Now there are varieties of gifts, but the same Spirit; and there are varieties of service, but the same Lord; and there are varieties of working, but it is the same God who inspires them all in every one.

For just as the body is one and has many members, and all the members of the body, though many, are one body, so it is with Christ. For by one Spirit we were all baptized into one body.

For the body does not consist of one member but of many. If the foot should say, "Because I am not a hand, I do not belong to the body," that would not make it any less a part of the body. And if the ear should say, "Because I am not an eye, I do not belong to the body," that would not make it any less a part of the body. If the whole body were an eye, where would be the hearing? If the whole body were an ear, where would be the sense

of smell? But as it is, God arranged the organs in the body, each one of them, as he chose. If one member suffers, all suffer together; if one member is honored, all rejoice together.

Now you are the body of Christ and individually members of it. And God has appointed in the church apostles, prophets, teachers, workers of miracles, healers, helpers, administrators, speakers in various tongues.

If I speak in the tongues of men and of angels, but have not love, I am a noisy gong or a clanging cymbal. And if I have prophetic powers, and understand all mysteries and all knowledge, and if I have all faith, so as to remove mountains, but have not love, I am nothing. If I give away all I have, and if I deliver my body to be burned, but have not love, I gain nothing.

Love is patient and kind; love is not jealous or boastful; it is not arrogant or rude. Love does not insist on its own way; it is not irritable or resentful; it does not rejoice at wrong, but rejoices in the right. Love bears all things, believes all things, hopes all things, endures all things.

Love never ends; as for prophecy, it will pass away; as for tongues, they will cease; as for knowledge, it will pass away. For our knowledge is imperfect and our prophecy is imperfect; but when the perfect comes, the imperfect will pass away. When I was a child, I spoke like a child, I thought like a child, I reasoned like a child; when I became a man, I gave up childish ways. For now we see in a mirror dimly, but then face to face. Now I know in part; then I shall understand fully, even as I have been fully understood. So faith, hope, love abide, these three; but the greatest of these is love.

Make love your aim, and earnestly desire the spiritual gifts. Be watchful, stand firm in your faith, be courageous, be strong. Let all that you do be done in love.
From 1 Corinthians 12: 4-6, 12-18, 26-28; 13: 1-13; 14: 1; 16: 13-14.

From Paul to the Galatians

I am astonished that you are so quickly deserting him who called you in the grace of Christ and turning to a different gospel. For I would have you know, brethren, that the gospel which was preached by me is not man's gospel. I did not receive it from man, nor was I taught it, but it came through a revelation of Jesus Christ.

In Christ Jesus you are all sons of God, through faith. There is neither Jew nor Greek, there is neither slave nor free, there is neither male nor female; for you are all one in Christ Jesus.

You were called to freedom, brethren; but through love be servants of one another. For the whole law is fulfilled in one word, "You shall love your neighbor as yourself." The fruit of the Spirit is love, joy, peace, patience, kindness, goodness, faithfulness, gentleness, self-control; against such there is no law. Let us have no self-conceit, no provoking of one another, no envy of one another. Bear one another's burdens, and so fulfil the law of Christ.

From Galatians 1: 6, 11–12; 3: 26, 28; 5: 13–14, 22–23, 26; 6: 2.

From Paul to the Ephesians

Blessed be the God and Father of our Lord Jesus Christ, who has blessed us in Christ with every spiritual blessing. He destined us in love to be his sons through Jesus Christ.

Because I have heard of your faith in the Lord Jesus and your love toward all the saints, I do not cease to give thanks for you, remembering you in my prayers.

For this reason I bow my knees before the Father, from whom every family in heaven and on earth is named, that according to the riches of his glory he may grant you to be strengthened with might through his Spirit in the inner man, and that Christ may dwell in your hearts through faith; that you, being rooted and grounded in love, may have power to comprehend with all the saints what is the breadth and length and height and depth, and to know the love of Christ which surpasses knowledge, that you may be filled with all the fulness of God.

I therefore, a prisoner for the Lord, beg you to lead a life worthy of the calling to which you have been called, with all lowliness and meekness, with patience, forbearing one another in love, eager to maintain the unity of the Spirit in the bond of peace. There is one body and one Spirit, just as you were called to the one hope that belongs to your call, one Lord, one faith, one baptism, one God and Father of us all, who is above all and through all and in all.

Therefore, putting away falsehood, let every one speak the truth with his neighbor, for we are members one of another. Let all bitterness and wrath and anger and clamor and slander be put away from you, with all malice, and be kind to one another, tenderhearted, forgiving one another, as God in Christ forgave you.

From Ephesians 1: 3, 5, 15–16; 3: 14–19; 4: 1–6, 25, 31–32.

From Paul to the Philippians

Grace to you and peace from God our Father and the Lord Jesus Christ.

I thank my God in all my remembrance of you, always in every prayer of mine for you all making my prayer with joy, thankful for your partnership in the gospel from the first day until now. And I am sure that he who began a good work in you will bring it to completion at the day of Jesus Christ.

Rejoice in the Lord always; again I will say, Rejoice. Let all men know your forbearance. The Lord is at hand. Have no anxiety about anything, but in everything by prayer and supplication with thanksgiving let your requests be made known to God. And the peace of God, which passes all understanding, will keep your hearts, and your minds in Christ Jesus.

Finally, brethren, whatever is true, whatever is honorable, whatever is just, whatever is pure, whatever is lovely, whatever is gracious, if there is any excellence, if there is anything worthy of praise, think about these things. What you have learned and heard and seen in me, do; and the God of peace will be with you.

From Philippians 1: 2–6; 4: 4–9.

From Paul to Timothy

To Timothy, my true child in the faith:

Grace, mercy, and peace from God the Father and Christ Jesus our Lord.

I urge that supplications, prayers, intercessions, and thanksgivings be made for all men, for kings and all who are in high positions, that we may lead a quiet and peaceable life, godly and respectful in every way. This is good, and it is acceptable in the sight of God our Savior, who desires all men to be saved and to come to the knowledge of the truth. For there is one God, and there

249

is one mediator between God and men, the man Christ Jesus, who gave himself as a ransom for all. For this I was appointed a preacher and apostle, a teacher of the Gentiles in faith and truth.

I thank God when I remember you constantly in my prayers. I long night and day to see you, that I may be filled with joy. I am reminded of your sincere faith, a faith that dwelt first in your grandmother Lo'is and your mother Eunice and now, I am sure, dwells in you. Hence I remind you to rekindle the gift of God that is within you through the laying on of my hands; for God did not give us a spirit of timidity but a spirit of power and love and self-control.

Do not be ashamed then of testifying to our Lord, nor of me his prisoner, but take your share of suffering for the gospel in the power of God. Follow the pattern of the sound words which you have heard from me, in the faith and love which are in Christ Jesus; guard the truth that has been entrusted to you by the Holy Spirit.

Continue in what you have learned and have firmly believed, knowing from whom you learned it and how from childhood you have been acquainted with the sacred writings which are able to instruct you for salvation through faith in Christ Jesus. All scripture is inspired by God and profitable for teaching, for reproof, for correction, and for training in righteousness, that the man of God may be complete, equipped for every good work.

For I am already on the point of being sacrificed; the time of my departure has come. I have fought the good fight, I have finished the race, I have kept the faith. Henceforth there is laid up for me the crown of righteousness, which the Lord, the righteous judge, will award to me on that Day, and not only to me but also to all who have loved his appearing.

The Lord will rescue me from every evil and save me for his heavenly kingdom. To him be the glory for ever and ever. Amen.

From 1 Timothy 1: 2; 2: 1–7; 2 Timothy 1: 3–8, 13–14; 3: 14–17; 4: 6–8, 18.

From Letters of James, Peter, and John

Count it all joy, my brethren, when you meet various trials, for you know that the testing of your faith produces steadfastness. And let steadfastness have its full effect, that you may be perfect and complete.

If any of you lacks wisdom, let him ask God who gives to all men generously and without reproaching, and it will be given him. But let him ask in faith, with no doubting, for he who doubts is like a wave of the sea that is driven and tossed by the wind. For that person must not suppose that a double-minded man, unstable in all his ways, will receive anything from the Lord.

Blessed is the man who endures trial, for when he has stood the test he will receive the crown of life which God has promised to those who love him. Let no one say when he is tempted, "I am tempted by God"; for God cannot be tempted with evil and he himself tempts no one; but each person is tempted when he is lured and enticed by his own desire. Then desire when it has conceived gives birth to sin; and sin when it is full-grown brings forth death.

Do not be deceived, my beloved brethren. Every good endowment and every perfect gift is from above, coming down from the Father of lights with whom there is no variation or shadow due to change. Of his own will he

251

brought us forth by the word of truth that we should be a kind of first fruits of his creatures.

Let every man be quick to hear, slow to speak, slow to anger, for the anger of man does not work the righteousness of God. Therefore put away all filthiness and rank growth of wickedness and receive with meekness the implanted word, which is able to save your souls.

But be doers of the word, and not hearers only, deceiving yourselves. For if any one is a hearer of the word and not a doer, he is like a man who observes his natural face in a mirror; for he observes himself and goes away and at once forgets what he was like. But he who looks into the perfect law, the law of liberty, and perseveres, being no hearer that forgets but a doer that acts, he shall be blessed in his doing.

If any one thinks he is religious, and does not bridle his tongue but deceives his heart, this man's religion is vain. Religion that is pure and undefiled before God and the Father is this: to visit orphans and widows in their affliction, and to keep oneself unstained from the world.

From James 1: 2–8, 12–27.

Beloved, do not be surprised at the fiery ordeal which comes upon you to prove you, as though something strange were happening to you. But rejoice in so far as you share Christ's sufferings, that you may also rejoice and be glad when his glory is revealed. If you are reproached for the name of Christ, you are blessed, because the spirit of glory and of God rests upon you. But let none of you suffer as a murderer, or a thief, or a wrongdoer, or a mischief-maker; yet if one suffers as a Christian, let him not be ashamed, but under that name

let him glorify God. And after you have suffered a little
while, the God of all grace, who has called you to his
eternal glory in Christ, will himself restore, establish, and
strengthen you. To him be the dominion for ever. Amen.

From 1 Peter 4: 12–16; 5: 10–11.

My little children, I am writing this to you so that
you may not sin; but if any one does sin, we have an advocate with the Father, Jesus Christ the righteous; and
he is the expiation for our sins, and not for ours only
but also for the sins of the whole world. And by this we
may be sure that we know him, if we keep his commandments. He who says "I know him" but disobeys his commandments is a liar, and the truth is not in him; but
whoever keeps his word, in him truly love for God is
perfected. By this we may be sure that we are in him:
he who says he abides in him ought to walk in the same
way in which he walked.

See what love the Father has given us, that we should be called children of God; and so we are.

If any one has the world's goods and sees his brother in need, yet closes his heart against him, how does God's love abide in him? Little children, let us not love in word or speech but in deed and in truth.

Beloved, let us love one another; for love is of God, and he who loves is born of God and knows God. He who does not love does not know God; for God is love. In this the love of God was made manifest among us, that God sent his only Son into the world, so that we might live through him. Beloved, if God so loved us, we also ought to love one another. No man has ever seen God; if we love one another, God abides in us and his love is perfected in us. There is no fear in love, but perfect love casts out fear. For fear has to do with punishment, and he who fears is not perfected in love.

We love, because he first loved us. If any one says, "I love God," and hates his brother, he is a liar; for he who does not love his brother whom he has seen, cannot love God whom he has not seen. And this commandment we have from him, that he who loves God should love his brother also.

From 1 John 2: 1–6; 3: 1, 17–18; 4: 7–9, 11–12, 18–21.

The Revelation to John

The revelation of Jesus Christ, which God gave him to show to his servants what must soon take place; and he made it known by sending his angel to his servant John, who bore witness to the word of God and to the testimony of Jesus Christ, even to all that he saw.

I John, was on the island called Patmos on account of

254

the word of God and the testimony of Jesus. I was in the Spirit on the Lord's day, and I heard behind me a loud voice saying, "Write what you see in a book."

From Revelation 1: 1–2, 9–11.

After this I looked, and lo, in heaven an open door! And the first voice, which I had heard speaking to me like a trumpet, said, "Come up hither, and I will show you what must take place after this." At once I was in the Spirit, and lo, a throne stood in heaven, with one seated on the throne! And round the throne, day and night, they never cease to sing,
"Holy, holy, holy, is the Lord God Almighty,
who was and is and is to come!
Worthy art thou, our Lord and God,
to receive glory and honor and power,
for thou didst create all things,
and by thy will they existed and were created."

From Revelation 4: 1–2, 8, 11.

After this I looked, and behold, a great multitude which no man could number, from every nation, from all tribes and peoples and tongues, standing before the throne and before the Lamb, clothed in white robes, with palm branches in their hands, and crying out with a loud voice, "Salvation belongs to our God who sits upon the throne, and to the Lamb!" And all the angels stood round the throne and round the elders, and they fell on their faces before the throne and worshiped God, saying, "Amen! Blessing and glory and wisdom and thanksgiving and honor and power and might be to our God for ever and ever! Amen."

Then I heard what seemed to be the voice of a great multitude, like the sound of many waters and like the sound of mighty thunderpeals, crying,

> "Hallelujah! For the Lord our God the Almighty
> reigns.
> Let us rejoice and exult and give him the glory."
>
> *From Revelation 7: 9–12; 19: 6–7.*

Then I saw a new heaven and a new earth; for the first heaven and the first earth had passed away, and the sea was no more. And I saw the holy city, new Jerusalem, coming down out of heaven from God, prepared as a bride adorned for her husband; and I heard a great voice from the throne saying, "Behold, the dwelling of God is with men. He will dwell with them, and they shall be his people, and God himself will be with them; he will wipe away every tear from their eyes, and death shall be no more, neither shall there be mourning nor crying nor pain any more, for the former things have passed away."

And I saw no temple in the city, for its temple is the Lord God the Almighty and the Lamb. And the city has no need of sun or moon to shine upon it, for the glory of God is its light, and its lamp is the Lamb. By its light shall the nations walk; and the kings of the earth shall bring their glory into it, and its gates shall never be shut by day—and there shall be no night there; they shall bring into it the glory and the honor of the nations.

From Revelation 21: 1–4, 22–26.